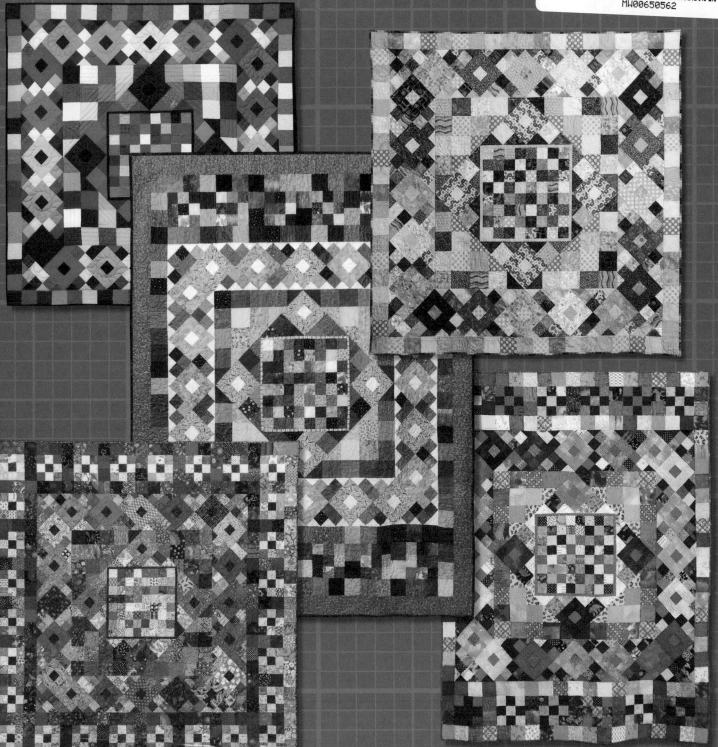

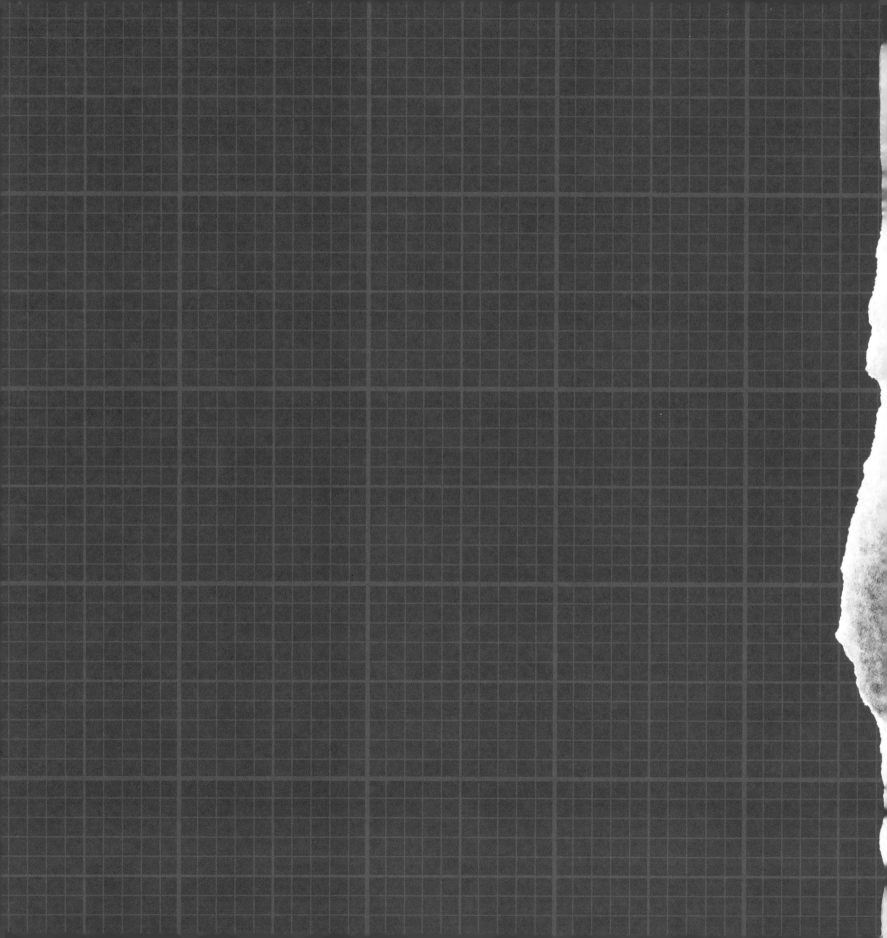

BRICKS cobblestones AND PEBBLES

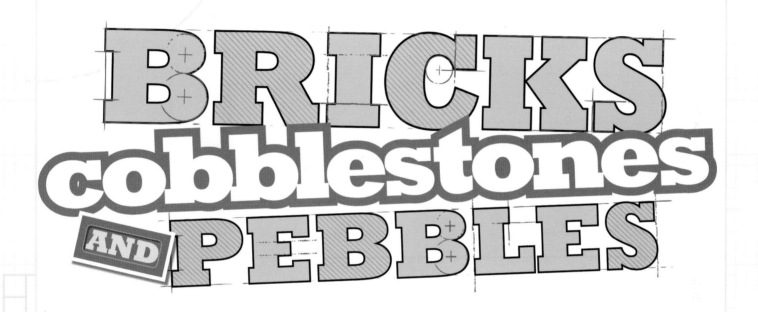

A PATH TO MODERN QUILTS

GYLEEN X. FITZGERALD

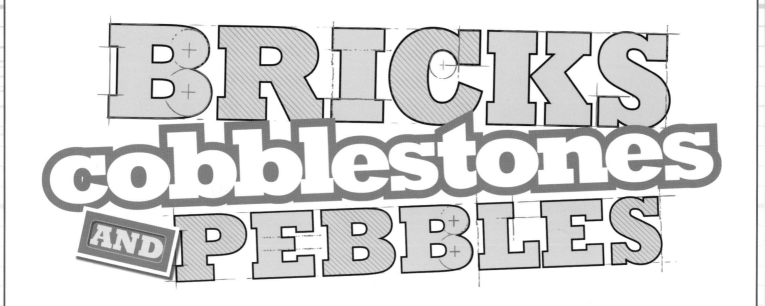

BRICKS cobblestones AND PEBBLES

A PATH TO MODERN QUILTS

GYLEEN X. FITZGERALD

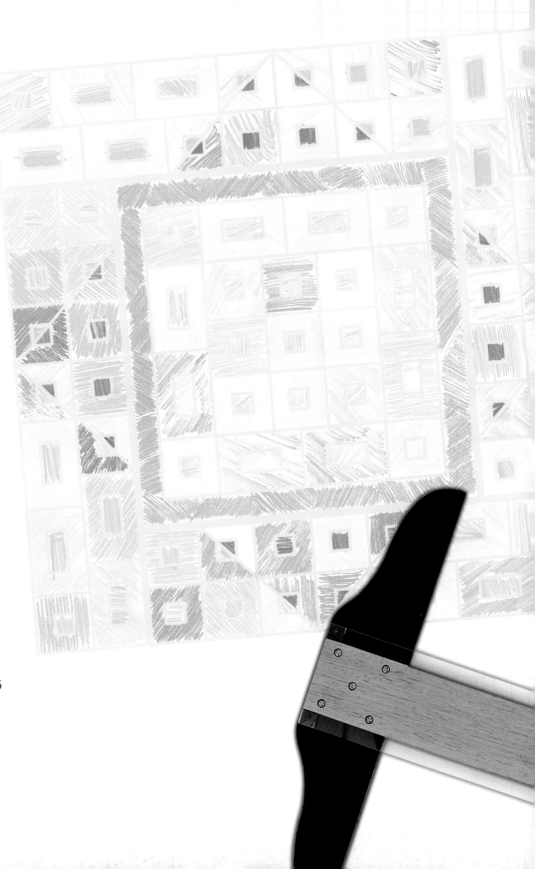

 **FPI Publishing**

P.O. Box 247
Havre de Grace, MD 21078
www.ColourfulStitches.com

Book Design: Brian Boehm
Cover Design: Brian Boehm
Pattern Layout: Brian Boehm
Studio Photography: Raymond C.H. McGowan
Text Editor: Gail F. Johnson
Pattern Editor: Gail Evans Tilton
Copy Editor: Gail F. Johnson

ISBN: 978-0-9768215-8-8

LIBRARY OF CONGRESS CONTROL NUMBER: 2016906965

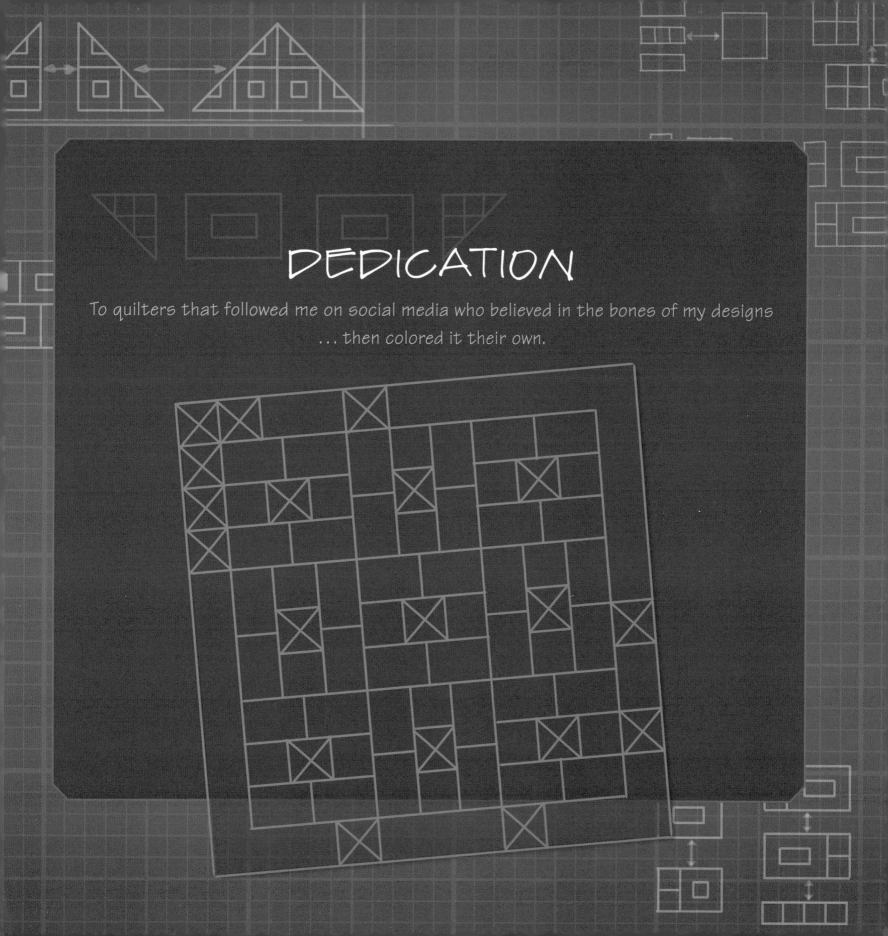

DEDICATION

To quilters that followed me on social media who believed in the bones of my designs
... then colored it their own.

PREFACE

I'm inspired by the geometry of a square. The square shows up in life in myriad forms: from patio pavers to modern architecture to floor tiles. I can't recall how many times I've been in a hotel bathroom and begun sketching the tile work on the floor and walls. Even on casual walks through new cities, I'd stop and ponder what's before me; then the sketching would start. It's a shape that just won't leave me alone…be done…over with!

The square, one of the fundamental shapes of geometry, is a building block for a multitude of other shapes. I, armed with a camera, or more likely my smart phone, recorded the patterns made with squares during my travels through France, Italy, Ireland and major cities in the United States. Churches, courtyards, town centers, public parks, even my own back yard provide frameworks for building a quilt. The square can appear huge or small, sometimes elongated or truncated, and then divided into triangles.

Obsessed, and brimming with a plethora of ideas, I sketched and stitched quilts. *Bricks, Cobblestones and Pebbles* came to life. I explored the square through its many variations. Contemporary designs with moderate piecing viewed through a barrage of color. Modern designs with limited piecing echoing clean lines and a bold presence. Scrappy designs because, my heavens, how did I get so much stuff! Scrappy is full of complexity, with a warmth of texture.

The square, simplistic yet powerful in form, became the building block of the 21 "blueprints" for the quilt designs in *Bricks, Cobblestones and Pebbles*. I, rooted in traditional quiltmaking, known for contemporary quilts, was firmly paving a path to modern.

TABLE OF CONTENTS

9   INTRODUCTION

11   TOOLS OF THE TRADE

13   DESIGN MASTER CLASS

17   CONSTRUCTION MASTER CLASS

29   QUILT BLUEPRINTS

137   THE SPECIALISTS

140   ACKNOWLEDGMENTS

143   ABOUT THE AUTHOR

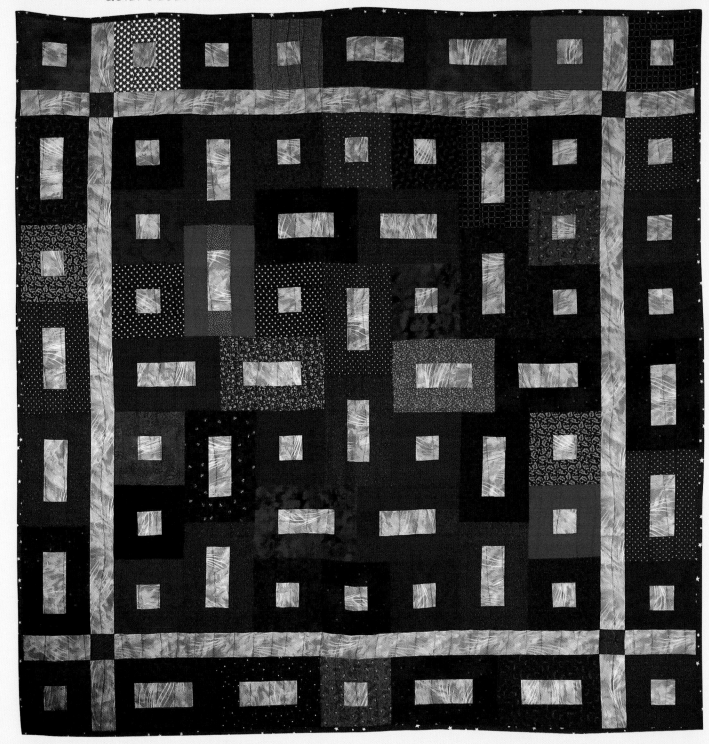

INTRODUCTION

Blueprint, a noun, is a design plan or other technical drawing. I consider it a guideline for building. To me, it doesn't matter if it's a house or a quilt, it's just a guide. Open to variation and personalization with consideration to budget and time on hand.

Each quilt blueprint in *Bricks, Cobblestones and Pebbles* is meant as a launching point for a contemporary, modern or scrap quilt. The choice is yours. You can mix and match components, use pre-cut strips or build from your stash, or start one way and end another… it's all okay. It's your quilt.

Feel free to jump straight to the designs or meander through the building matrix for component options. I've included a full line-drawn sketch of each design; this represents the "bones" of the design. Explore the possibilities of the design using colored pencils to create pieced borders or boundaries within the quilt. Once you get the knack of it, you can color an original.

I encourage you to begin where you are using what you have on hand. I cut and stitch as the quilt is being developed versus cutting for the entire quilt at the start. I've set up the patterns with this philosophy; hence full yardage is sometimes not given. This way when time runs out, I can stop and call it done. No evidence remains that the quilt should have been larger or different. It's a secret that stays in my studio. All the remaining fabric, uncut into pieces, can go back into the stash without me feeling remorse or guilt. Remember it is better to finish small than not to finish at all.

If you are a saver of scraps, or in my case a "store-r" of scraps, here is your opportunity to expand and stretch your coloring and fabric blending skills. Each blueprint can be made scrappy which will use up or put a dent in your 2½" Gravel, 3½" Pebble squares and 1½" Stick strips as well as your 2½" strips. Talk about cut and ready to go! From there all you need is time.

Quilting should be fun, inspiring and perhaps a bit challenging but never frustrating. Take it step-by-step following the blueprint of choice. Then step back; you've engineered a masterpiece!

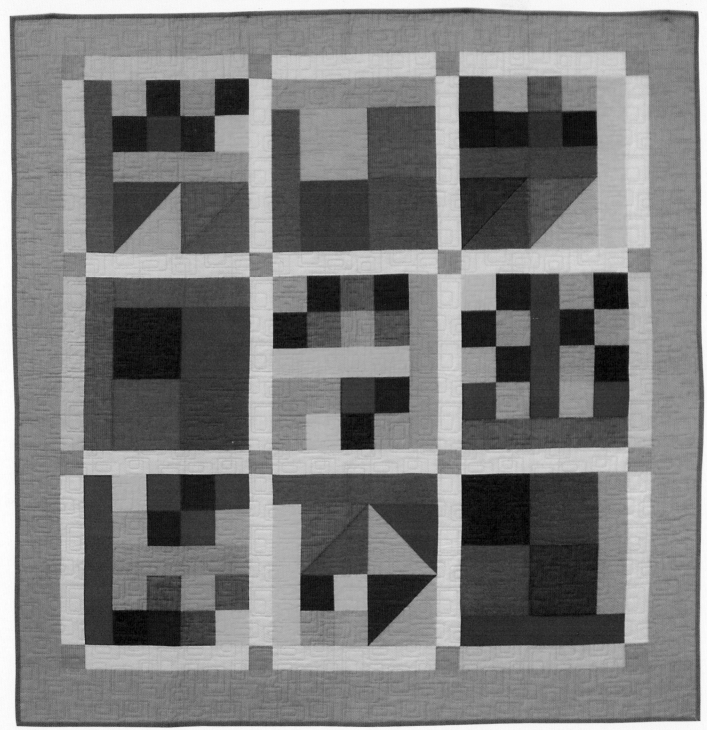

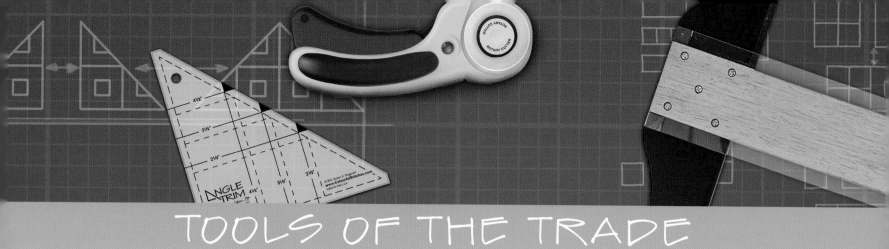

TOOLS OF THE TRADE

Planning is 80% of the work that makes piecing a breeze. Before you just jump in and start making quilts let's go through the basics or conventions used throughout *Bricks, Cobblestones and Pebbles*. I equate this with having the correct tools and supplies on hand before you begin a major construction project.

Having a series of standard rulers and supplies saves time and the frustration of just making do. I see them as tools in my quiltmaking toolbox. Is it time to do an inventory of what's in your toolbox?

50wt OR 60wt THREAD

Any high quality thread will work. I have a preference for Aurifil. I like its silky quality and long staple cotton fiber. You want a thread that doesn't produce much lint, if any. I also prefer one what is easy to "un-sew." I use two different colors, one in the top and one in the bobbin that I can see against the wrong side of my fabric. By doing this, it is easy to troubleshoot stitching problems because you will know if the bobbin or top thread has the irregular stitch. Most times just rethreading the top or re-installing the bobbin solves the problem.

While we are on the topic, all seams throughout *Bricks, Cobblestones and Pebbles* are sewn with a ¼" seam width; and I use between a 2.2 to 2.5mm stitch length. To get a close to accurate ¼" seam width, I align the fabric to the edge of my presser foot. Depending on what presser foot I'm using, I move the needle position so that it's a ¼" away. I'm not fond of using an edge guide on the presser foot. I'm not sure if I can consistently determine if the fabric is in the correct placement or is rolled against the guide or not close enough. Some find it easier to just mark the throat plate with tape or some other gadget; that works too. Take a moment to be Goldilocks and see what stitch length works with your machine that is not too small (used for paper piecing) or not too large (used for basting) but one that is just right ... for piecing. Don't forget to determine the position of your magic ¼" seam as well.

ROTARY CUTTER WITH A NEW BLADE

I know, I know…I don't change mine often and when I do I'm surprised each time how easy cutting through multiple layers of fabric can be. You would think that I would change the blade automatically between major quilt projects. Together, let's make this a new habit. The brand of cutter you choose is up to you; just remember to close or retract the blade when you're not cutting.

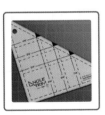

SPECIALTY RULERS AND TOOLS

Of course you are going to need an Angle Trim Tool for a few of the designs in *Bricks, Cobblestones and Pebbles*. The Angle Trim Tool was designed especially to handle "pieced" triangles. I also find it handy to have a 4½", 6½" and 8½" square ruler; any brand will do. I use these to "square up" or trim rough piecing to the exact size needed. The square rulers are not critical but certainly reduce errors when trying to find the middle and trim from four sides.

FABRIC

Building a stash or having just what is needed for the project is a personal choice. In theory, most quilts use a high quality 100% cotton fabric produced especially for quiltmaking. I give some flexibility on that theory. What you use is determined by what you have on hand, how you intend to use the quilt, your economic situation and your courage. Lately, I have been experimenting with Dupioni silk and linen when making quilts that will hang on the wall. I'm mixing them with 100% cotton quilting fabric. However, in the past I have used cotton/polyester blended fabric in a bed quilt because it was the perfect print, ample amount of yardage and I had it on hand. I'm not sure how long it will last so that is a risk but certainly it will outlast the 100% cotton and my lifetime. If you are using vintage or upcycled fabric make sure it has the integrity needed for the purpose of the quilt.

COLORED PENCILS OR PENS

Oh, what fun it is to create a virtual quilt. I do like to design on the fly with color and fabric; however, I don't always end with a result that is pleasing. I don't mind, and for sure I have my fair share of unusable blocks and strips. With *Bricks, Cobblestones and Pebbles*, I have included full sketches or "bones" of the design for you to color as you wish. This is a great way to get a sense of what the quilt will look like if you "go off the reservation" and try a new coloring. Nothing is wasted, you've limited your risk and knowledge is gained. How cool is that? I have a 24-pack of Crayola pencils. I got them at an office supply store and they are very inexpensive when you buy them at the beginning of the school year. Any brand of colored pencil or pens will work…Crayola is cheap enough that I don't get upset if I lose one.

DESIGN
MASTER CLASS

COLOR THEORY

Big topic…where do I start? For me color is about more than quality of light, medium and dark. It transcends the concepts of primary, secondary, triadic or complementary. It's bigger than that and it can become huge when you step outside of just using solids. Color to me is complex and each piece of fabric is relative or has its part only when standing with another fabric. It's dependent. The easiest way to explain this theory is to compare it to a church choir. Taking it voice by voice… here goes.

SOLOIST

This is the feature fabric and like a soloist will make your quilt sing. Think about the soloist as a large scale print; it could be a bold solid or a novelty fabric. However, too many soloists featured in one song causes disharmony and the song goes on and on and on, forever. Be wise; select only one to use in the quilt.

HARMONIZER

This is the voice that blends or goes between the soloist and the choir. You know, the voice that has range and can keep the peace. You hear this voice mostly when listening to a capella singers like a barbershop quartet. The harmonizer is standing between connecting the sound if you will. Think about the harmonizer as the fabric that can hold up to the most dominant soloist yet does not disappear when mixed among the choir. Black and white print and striped fabrics are wonderful harmonizers assuming you didn't use a similar fabric in the choir. Again, it's relative to what fabrics you plan to use. Keep your options open.

CHOIR

This is where you have the variety of both color and scale. These are the voices that are nice and even; great but for sure they are not "show off" soloists. The voices can stand in for each other or in fabric terms … when one fabric runs out you can use another fabric in its place without affecting the design. The size of the choir or the number of fabrics in the quilt adds depth and complexity to the quilt. Remember, a three-color quilt can have more than three fabrics! This is the bulk of my stash.

BACKGROUND

Every choir needs a stage that is sturdy enough to hold all the voices; a platform of sorts on which to perform. This is also true for quilt blocks. In traditional or contemporary quilt blocks there is the focus design and the support to that design called the background. It can also be considered as the "negative" space when you think of the coloring in modern quilt blocks. When selecting fabric you want something that does not compete with the choir or harmonizer or soloist. In most cases one fabric will do, however, a combination of fabrics that have the same voice or "read" the same will also work. Think of a collection of light fabric creating the support to dark, bright or even pastel fabric. It forms a clean line against those fabrics to define shape.

FINAL THOUGHTS

Nothing is absolute when talking about color or fabric. For me it is common in my scrap quilts to use a harmonizer and not use a soloist. Yet, in my contemporary quilts, I almost always use a soloist. I love to create modern quilts with contemporary block construction by using choir fabric that blends or vanishes against the background fabric.

The architectural designs in *Bricks, Cobblestones and Pebbles* stand strong with clean clear edges that are defined by color. Several of the designs that are built in rounds lend themselves to being treated like medallion quilts by changing the value from round to round. I love pieced borders or colored components that can mimic a one fabric border.

In most of the patterns I have included a full sketch or "bones" of the design. When experimenting, make several copies of the sketch and color the components to create a structure that looks visually original. Know that it is more than accepted to end with coloring which makes your quilt unique. Think of it as a planned housing sub-division. The bones of all the houses are made from just a few designs yet look unique unto themselves within the community. Personalize through coloring.

QUILT BLUEPRINT: COBBLESTONES   MADE AND QUILTED BY GYLEEN X. FITZGERALD

16

CONSTRUCTION
MASTER CLASS

Welcome to your "One-Stop-Shop" for building components.

This is a pick-what-you-need instead of the more familiar supply list. I tried to keep the matrix as simplified as possible without limiting your options. Given the bones or blueprint of the quilt you customize the outcome by selecting from the matrix. For example, you can replace all the Bricks in the blueprint with rectangles or if you're a collector or saver of scraps, you can use six Pebbles instead. They all fit in the same space which makes them interchangeable.

You can, of course, mix and match. I labeled the columns **Contemporary, Modern** and **Scrappy**, however don't let a mere label put you in a smaller box than you own! Just ignore the label and do what you feel is best for the blueprint, your fabric, the available time and your skill level. At the end you will be the Master Quilter!

BUILDING MATRIX

	CONTEMPORARY	MODERN	SCRAPPY
BRICKS	6½" x 9½"	6½" x 9½" RECTANGLE	6 PEBBLES
COBBLESTONES	6½" x 6½"	6½" x 6½" SQUARE	4 PEBBLES / 9 GRAVEL
PINWHEELS	8½"	6½"	4½" HALF-SQUARE TRIANGLE (HST)
PEBBLES 3½" SQUARE	1 PEBBLE	2 PEBBLES / 3½" x 6½" RECTANGLE	3 PEBBLES / 3½" x 9½" RECTANGLE
GRAVEL 2½" SQUARE	1 GRAVEL	4 GRAVEL	
STICKS	1½" STRIP		

THE MAKING OF A BRICK

How much do I need?

- For one Brick you need two fabrics, 2½" x 24" for the Brick and 2½" x 5½" for the center. The fabric will be crosscut giving you the opportunity to use bits and pieces.

How do I make it?

- Using a 24" strip, cut (2) 2½" x 9½" and (2) 2½" x 2½" segments. Using another fabric, cut (1) 2½" x 5½" center.

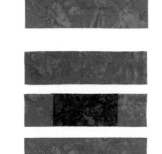

- Stitch the 2½" x 2½" squares to each end of the 2½" x 5½" center. Press seams to the square.

- Stitch (1) 2½" x 9½" segment to the assembly. Press seam to the segment.

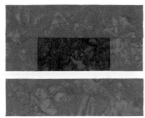

- Stitch the remaining 2½" x 9½" segment to the assembly. Press seam to the segment.

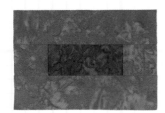

THE MAKING OF A COBBLESTONE

How much do I need?

- For one Cobblestone you need two fabrics, 2½" x 18" for the Cobblestone and 2½" x 2½" for the center. The fabric will be crosscut giving you the opportunity to use bits and pieces.

How do I make it?

- Using an 18" strip, cut (2) 2½" x 6½" and (2) 2½" x 2½" segments. Using another fabric, cut (1) 2½" x 2½" center.

- Stitch the 2½" x 2½" squares to each end of the 2½" x 2½" center. Press seams to the outside squares.

- Stitch (1) 2½" x 6½" segment to the assembly. Press seam to the segment.

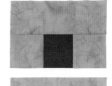

- Stitch the remaining 2½" x 6½" segment to the assembly. Press seam to the segment.

THE MAKING OF A PINWHEEL

Basic Construction

Lay out (4) Half-Square Triangles. Stitch (2) Half-Square Triangles together to form pairs. Press seams clockwise or counterclockwise following the rotation established.

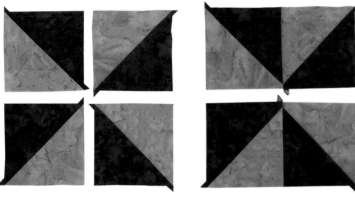

Stitch pairs together to complete the Pinwheel. Press continuing the rotation, clockwise or counter-clockwise.

Trim to size as needed. Yield one Pinwheel.

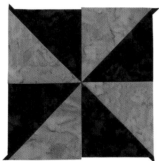

Front

Note: To spin the center remove center stitches in the seam allowance.

Back

8½" Pinwheel using 5" squares

How much do I need?

- (4) 5" squares, two from each of two fabrics. You can also use a 5" charm pack and mix the fabrics within your pinwheel.

How do I make it?

- Using (2) fabrics, cut (4) 5" x 5" squares, (2) from each fabric.
- Draw a diagonal line corner to corner on the wrong side of the lighter fabric. Pair the fabric, one of each, with right sides together.

- Stitch ¼" on both sides of the diagonal line. Cut apart on the marked line. Press seams to the darker fabric. Yields (4) Half-Square Triangles.

 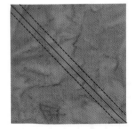

- Continue following the basic construction.

6½" Pinwheel using 3½" Pebbles

How much do I need?

- (8) 3½" Pebbles in two fabrics, four of each.

How do I make it?

- Using (2) fabrics, cut (4) 3½" x 3½" squares from each fabric.

Note: The 8½" Pinwheel uses 4½" squares.

- Draw a diagonal line corner to corner on the wrong side of the lighter fabric. Pair the fabric, one of each, with right sides together.

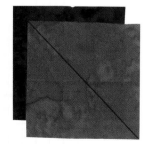

- Stitch on the diagonal marked line. Trim to ¼" from the diagonally marked line. Press seams to the darker fabric. Yields (4) Half-Square Triangles.

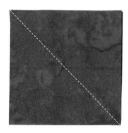

- Continue following the basic construction.

6½" Pinwheel using 3½" Strip

How much do I need?

- You need (1) 3½" strip by width of fabric from two fabrics.

How do I make it?

- Using 3½" strip from (2) fabrics, cut each fabric into Triangles using the Angle Trim Tool. Cut (4) Triangles from each fabric.

Note: The 8½" Pinwheel uses 4½" strips.

- Pair Triangles, one of each fabric, right sides together to form pairs. Stitch the diagonal edge using ¼" seam allowance. Press seam to the darker fabric. Yields (4) Half-Square Triangles.

- Continue following the basic construction.

TRIANGLES.

When you take a square and divide it in half diagonally from corner to opposite corner you get two triangles (in quilting, known as the Half-Square Triangle). Triangles are common in the masonry work found in buildings, walkways and, of course, tile work. Its basic geometry makes it a fun addition to *Bricks, Cobblestones and Pebbles.*

The **Angle Trim Tool** makes cutting Triangles for Half-Square Triangles or Pieced Triangles quick and accurate.

The solid lines are for raw edge alignment and the dash lines are for seam alignment.

Triangles 6½", 4½", 3½" or 2½"

USING SQUARES

(Step-outs illustrate 3½" Triangle)

- Cut square 6½" x 6½", 4½" x 4½", 3½" Pebble or 2½" Gravel

- With square right side up, place the bottom of the Angle Trim Tool on the bottom edge of the square [A]. Align the left edge of the square with the solid line on the toll representing the square size [B]. The top corner of the square will be even with the bottom edge of the dark triangle on the Angle Trim Tool [C].

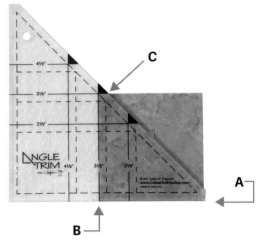

- Trim diagonal edge.

- Discard scrap trimmings.

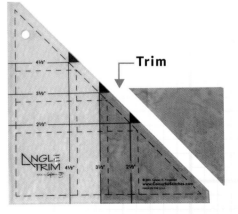

USING STRIPS

(Step-outs illustrate 3½" Triangle)

- Cut strip 6½", 4½", 3½" or 2½" by width of fabric.

- With right side of fabric facing up, place the bottom of the Angle Trim Tool on the bottom edge of the strip [A]. Align the left edge of the strip with the solid line on the tool representing the height of the strip [B]. The top corner of the strip will be even with the bottom edge of the dark triangle on the Angle Trim Tool [C].

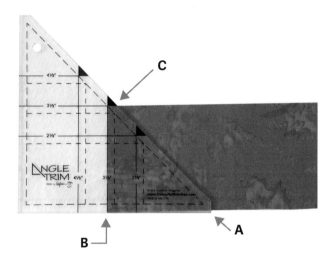

- Trim the diagonal edge first then the trim tip even with tool.

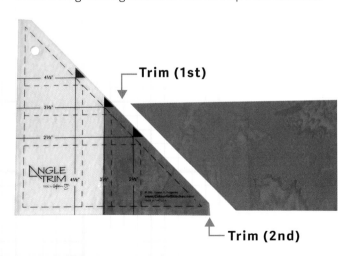

- Flip the Angle Trim Tool and reposition. Align the diagonal edge of the tool with the diagonal cut edge of the fabric [A]. The flat tip of the tool is even with the bottom edge of the fabric [B]. The top edge of the fabric is even with the solid line representing the height of the strip [C].

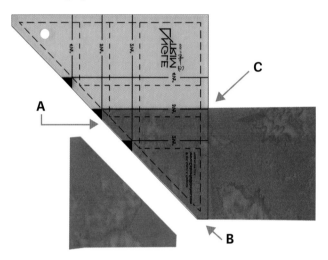

- Trim even with the edge of the tool.

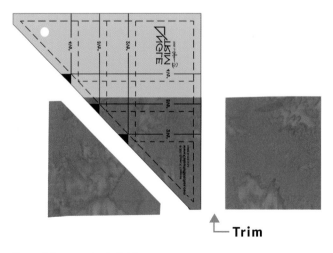

- Repeat for required yield.

THE MAKING OF (2) HALF-COBBLESTONES

How much do I need?

- You need (1) Brick.

How do I make it?

- Start with a Brick. With the Brick, right side up, place the Angle Trim Tool on the top-left of the Brick. Align seam lines with the dash lines on the tool. Trim.

- Rotate Angle Trim Tool and position on top-right of the Brick. Align seam lines with the dash lines on the tool. Trim.

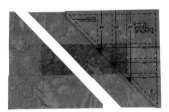 

- Discard center strip as scrap. Yield two Half-Cobblestones.

THE MAKING OF A HALF-COBBLESTONE

How much do I need?

- You need (1) Cobblestone.

How do I make it?

- Start with a Cobblestone. With the Cobblestone, right side up, place the Angle Trim Tool on the top-left of the Cobblestone. Align seam lines with the dash lines on the tool. Trim.

 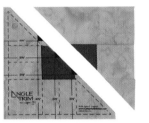

- Discard remaining as scrap. Yield one Half-Cobblestone.

MAKING OF A 6½" PIECED TRIANGLE WITH PEBBLES

How much do I need?

- You will need (3) Pebbles.

How do I make it?

- Cut (3) 3½" x 3½" Pebble squares from an assortment of fabric. Lay out the Pebbles in columns following the sketch.

- Stitch (2) Pebbles together from the 1st column. Press seam up.

- Stitch the Pebble in the 2nd column to the right of the first column. Press seam toward the 2nd column.

- With the assembly, right side up, place the Angle Trim Tool on top of the assembly. Align left and bottom edge of the Pebbles with the tool. Align seam lines with the dash lines on the tool. Trim.

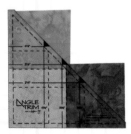

- Discard scrap trimmings. Yield one 6½" Pieced Triangle.

MAKING OF A 6½" PIECED TRIANGLE WITH GRAVEL

How much do I need?

- You will need (6) Gravel.

How do I make it?

- Cut (6) 2½" x 2½" Gravel squares from an assortment of fabric. Lay out the Gravel in columns following the sketch.

- Stitch (3) and (2) Gravel squares together from the 1st and 2nd columns, respectively. Press seam up for the 1st column and down for the 2nd column.

- Stitch 2nd to the right side of the 1st column. Add the Gravel, 3rd Column to the right of the 2nd column. Press seams toward the 3rd column.

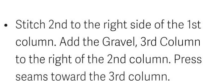

- With the assembly, right side up, place the Angle Trim Tool on top of the assembly. Align left and bottom edge of the Gravel with the tool. Align seam lines with the dash lines on the tool. Trim.

- Discard scrap trimmings. Yield one 6½" Pieced Triangle.

Here is a handy table of the types of Pieced Triangles that can be made from basic building components.

	BEFORE	WITH TOOL	AFTER
BRICKS			
COBBLESTONES			
PEBBLES 3½" SQUARE			
GRAVEL 2½" SQUARE			

QUILT BLUEPRINTS can look daunting and super complex as far as knowing where you start and how you assemble the quilt. The first thing I ask is, can rows or columns be established? If yes, I start to break down the blueprint into rows or columns then into sub-elements or blocks. Once I reach the smallest element that is where I start the piecing. Life is good.

However, if the answer is no, I can't establish rows or columns, that is when quiltmaking gets tricky. Not hard…just tricky. That is when I know a special seam is needed. In *Bricks, Cobblestones and Pebbles* that special seam is a partial seam. Life just got better.

Typically in traditional piecing, components form rows and columns. A partial seam is used when components surround a central element. Remember, a partial seam may not be needed for every seam, perhaps just for a sub-component assembly. Think tricky, not hard, and life becomes exciting.

Let me illustrate using four 6½" x 9½" rectangles and a Pebble.

Lay out components following the sketch.

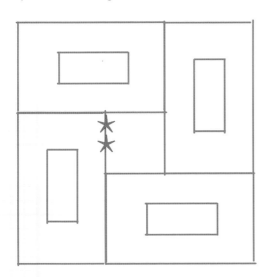

Start the partial seam at the ** notation. Stitch these two components together down half the distance of the smaller component. Stop. Press seam away from the center component.

Going in a clockwise direction, stitch the next component to the assembly. Stitch down the entire distance. Press seam away from the center component.

Continue in a clockwise direction stitching each outside component in turn. Press seam away from the center component.

Now complete the partial seam. Start stitching by overlapping 2-3 stitches. Then stitch to the end of the components. Press seam away from the center component.

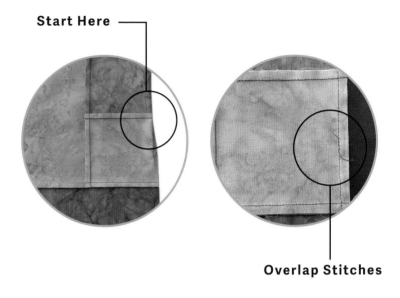

Start Here

Overlap Stitches

QUILT BLUEPRINTS

31	KEW GARDENS		79	TRIO
35	ENGLISH GARDEN		83	CITY HALL
39	FIVE AND CHANGE		87	SO SQUARE
43	WEAVER		93	ZIP ZAP
49	SCRAPPY COBBLESTONES		99	INSIDE OUT, INKED!
53	BUST THOSE SCRAPS!		103	SYMMETRY SQUARE
57	SQUARE TURN		109	RHYME AND REASON
61	I'VE GOT THIS		115	MAIN STREET COMMON
65	INNER CITY		125	ODDS, ENDS AND LEFTOVERS
71	UPTOWN		131	PICK UP STICKS
75	SMALL PLATES — QUILT TAPAS			

KEW GARDENS

Kew Gardens has a gentle transition from the pale Cobblestone border entry to the more intense center Pebbles. The Bricks create a pathway through the gardens' Soloist fabric as if on a leisurely stroll. Here's **Kew Gardens** as I remember it on that misty day in London.

SUPPLIES

- (17) 2½" x 40" strips in assorted Dark fabrics
- (15-20) 2½" x 40" strips in assorted Light fabrics
- (48) 3½" x 3½" Pebbles in assorted Dark fabrics
- 1 yard Soloist fabric for segments and binding

COMPONENT	QUANTITY
BRICKS	**16** (DARK)
COBBLESTONES	**28** (LIGHT)
3½" PEBBLES	**48** (DARK)

For Each Brick

- From (1) 2½" Dark strip, crosscut (2) 2½" x 9½" and (2) 2½" x 2½" segments.

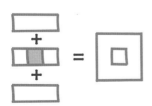

- From a 2½" Soloist strip, crosscut (1) 2½" x 5½" segment.

For Each Cobblestone

- From (1) 2½" Light strip, crosscut (2) 2½" x 6½" and (2) 2½" x 2½" segments.
- From a 2½" Soloist strip, crosscut (1) 2½" x 2½" segment.

INSTRUCTIONS

Round A, Center

1. Pair 3½" Pebbles by twos for (24) units; sew together and press seams to one side.

2. Using (8) pairs, stitch together by twos for (4) 4-Patches. Stitch 4-Patches together to form a 16-Patch Pebble center.

Round B, Border

3. Sew (1) 3½" pair unit to each Brick and press seams toward the Bricks. Make (16).

Make (16)

4. Sew together as follows to make Unit As. Make (4), Unit A1, A2, A3, A4.

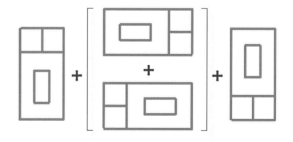

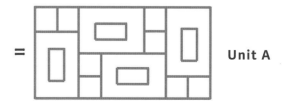

Unit A

5. Lay out (4) Unit As around the center.

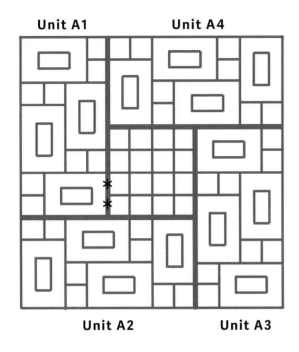

Unit A1   **Unit A4**

Unit A2   **Unit A3**

6. Stitch Unit A1 to Round A with a partial seam (**). Stitch together for about 4".

7. Stitch Unit A2 to Round A; this seam will include the end of the Unit A1 and the entire length of Round A.

9. Continue counterclockwise with Unit A3 and Unit A4.

10. Now complete the partial seam of Unit A1.

Round C, Border

11. Using (12) Cobblestones, stitch (6) end to end (rotating to avoid matching seams). Make (2) side border units.

12. Stitch a side border unit to left and right sides of Round B.

13. Using (16) Cobblestones, stitch (8) end to end (rotating the block to avoid matching seams). Make (2) border units.

14. Stitch border units to top and bottom of Round B.

15. Layer backing, batting and quilt top. Quilt as desired.

16. Make binding by connecting 2½" Soloist strips end-to-end with diagonal seams until the length is 12" longer than the distance around the quilt top. Fold and press in half lengthwise for a double binding. Sew binding to quilt.

17. Make a label to identify this quilt as being your art and enjoy!

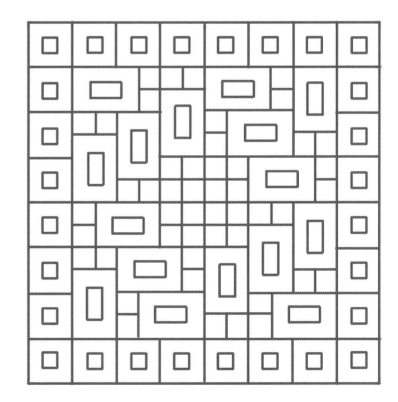

BABY'S GOT BACK

When you're on a roll it's easy to make a few more Cobblestone blocks. I make extras so I have plenty of options to audition for the front of the quilt. I incorporate the "rejects" into the quilt backs. Here I used the reject Cobblestones for the cornerstones…and the lightest became my label. Done. Pretty cool, huh?

COMPONENTS	SIZE	QUANTITY
BLOCKS	15" X 15"	9
SASHING	6½" X 15"	12
COBBLESTONES	6½" X 6½"	4

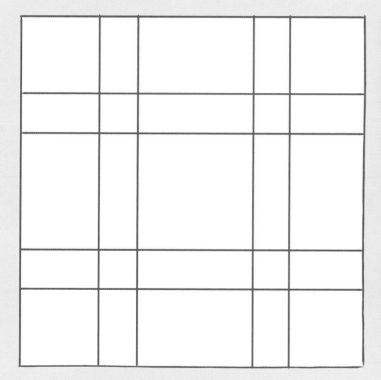

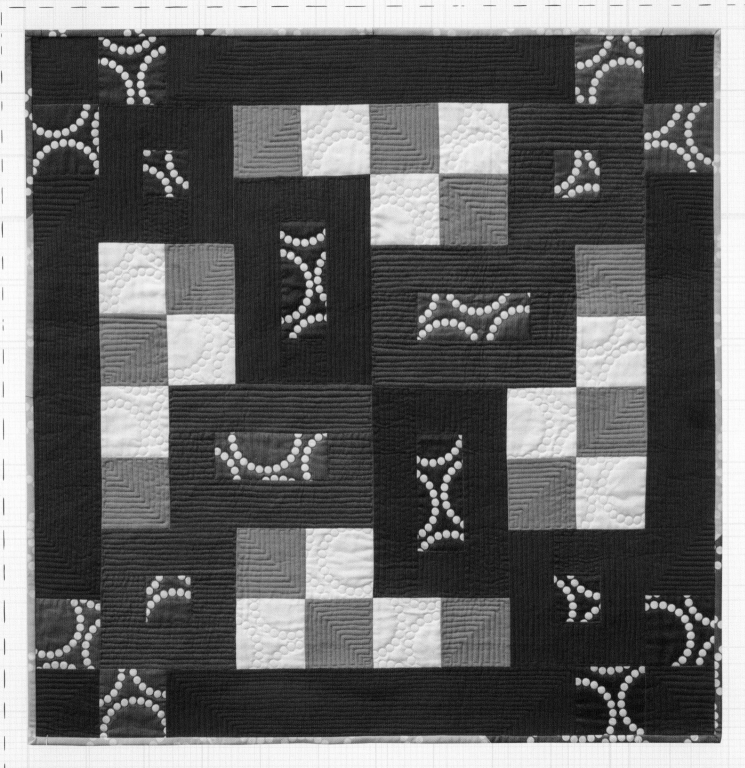

ENGLISH GARDEN

Inspired by a flower garden in London, England, I sketched **English Garden**. A huge flower, demanding to be noticed, took center stage as I remembered it. That image is represented by the four central Bricks. Enter Charlotte Noll. I asked Charlotte to use the **English Garden** design for a "Modern" quilt. She and her friend, Debby colored the design to make a big "modern X," hence the title of Charlotte's quilt, "Debby's Modern X." Charlotte said, she quilted it with free motion modern organic straight lines and stitched around the pearls. "I like this quilting because it's not perfect and gives it an interesting texture." True to form, each quilter can make a quilt her own and still be within the architectural "bones" of the original design.

SUPPLIES

- (1 or 2) 18" x 22" Soloist fabric
- (4) 18" x 22" in assorted Choir fabrics
- ¼ yard border fabric
- ¼ yard binding fabric

COMPONENT	QUANTITY
BRICKS	4
COBBLESTONES	4
3½" PEBBLES	36

For Each Brick

- From (1) Choir fabric, cut (2) 2½" strips; crosscut (2) 2½" x 9½" and (2) 2½" x 2½" segments.
- From (1) Soloist fabric, cut (1) 2½" strip; crosscut (1) 2½" x 5½" segment.
- Make (4) Bricks using (2) Choir and (1-2) Soloist fabrics.

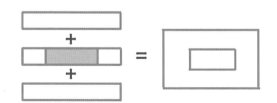

For Each Cobblestone

- From (1) Choir fabric, cut (2) 2½" strips; crosscut (2) 2½" x 6½" and (2) 2½" x 2½" segments.
- From (1) Soloist fabric, cut (1) 2½" strip; crosscut (1) 2½" x 2½" square.
- Make (4) Cobblestones using (2) Choir and (1-2) Soloist fabrics.

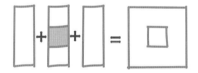

For Each Pebble

- Using (2) Choir fabrics, cut (12) 3½" x 3½" squares from each fabric.
- Using (1-2) Soloist fabrics, cut (8) 3½" x 3½" squares.

INSTRUCTIONS

1. Stitch (2) 3½" Choir Pebbles together to make (16) Pebble pairs.

2. Using (8) Choir Pebble pairs, stitch (2) together to make 4-Patch. Make (4).

3. Stitch 4-Patch to Cobblestone. Make (4) Unit A.

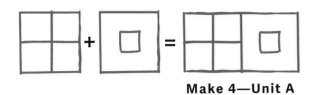

Make 4—Unit A

4. Using (4). Choir Pebble pairs, stitch to Brick. Make (4) Unit B.

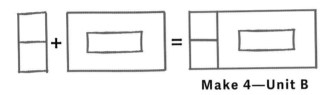

Make 4—Unit B

5. Stitch Unit A to Unit B following sketch, make (4) blocks.

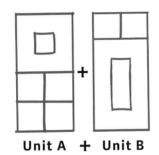

Unit A + Unit B

6. Lay out blocks 2 across and 2 down, with Bricks meeting in the center (see full sketch at right).

7. Stitch together block to block to form rows. Then row to row to complete the center.

8. Using the border fabric, cut (4) 3½" x 24½" strips and (4) 3½" x 3½" Pebbles.

9. Using (1) border strip and (2) 3½" Soloist Pebbles, stitch (1) Pebble to each end of strip. Make (2) border units.

10. Stitch (1) border unit to each side of center.

11. Using (1) border strip, (2) Soloist Pebbles and (2) border Pebbles, stitch Soloist and border Pebbles together to form pairs. Then stitch (1) pair to each end of border strip with the border Pebble on the ends. Make (2) border units.

12. Stitch border unit to top and bottom of center.

13. Layer backing, batting and quilt top. Quilt as desired.

14. Make binding by connecting 2½" strips of binding fabric end-to-end with diagonal seams until the length is 12" longer than the distance around the quilt top. Fold and press in half lengthwise for a double binding. Sew binding to quilt.

15. Make a label to identify this quilt as being your art and attach a sleeve for hanging. Enjoy.

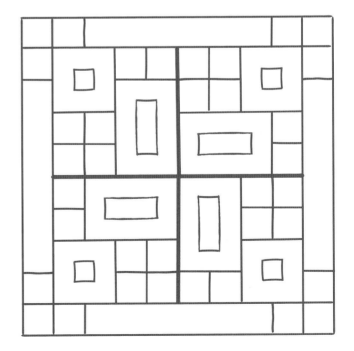

THINK MODULAR

- Make (9) centers, steps 1-7.

- Make (24) border strips, steps 8-9, to use as sashing between the centers and as a framing border.

- Cut (16) 3½" x 3½" border Pebbles to use as cornerstones between the sashing/border strips.

FIVE AND CHANGE

Clean lines and graphic impact describe the bones of this design. It's made from 5" charm squares and scraps or sticks of fabric "change." Judy made two samples and faster than you can say, "BAM!" they were finished.

SUPPLIES

- (24) 1½" x 40" strips in assorted light fabric
- (24) 1½" x 40" strips in assorted dark fabric
- (32) 5" x 5" squares in assorted light (Fabric A) with at least (2) squares per fabric*
- (32) 5" x 5" squares in assorted dark (Fabric B) with at least (2) squares per fabric*
- ⅔ yards binding fabric

*NOTE: ½ yard (cut into (32) 5" squares) if using one fabric for light or dark squares.

Using the 1½" x 40" strips, crosscut the following

STRIPS	LIGHT	DARK
1½" x 4½"	64	
1½" x 5½"	64	
1½" x 10½"		32
1½" x 12½"		32

INSTRUCTIONS

1. Select (2) 5" squares of (1) Fabric A and (2) 5" squares of (1) Fabric B. Mark a diagonal line on the wrong side of Fabric A. Pair together one light and one dark with right sides together. Stitch ¼" from BOTH sides of the diagonal line. Make (4) Half-Square Triangles.

2. Cut apart on the diagonal line and press towards the dark triangle. Trim each Half-Square Triangle to 4½" x 4½".

3. Select (4) 1½" x 4½" strips. Stitch to (1) each Half-Square Triangle from step 2. Follow the sketch for placement. Press toward the strip. Make (4).

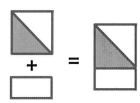

4. Select (4) 1½" x 5½" strips. Stitch (1) to each Half-Square Triangle. Follow the sketch for placement. Press toward the strip. Make (4).

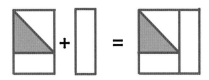

5. Lay out (4) pieced Half-Square Triangle units following sketch. Stitch (2) together to form pairs. Finally, stitch pairs together to form a sashed Pinwheel.

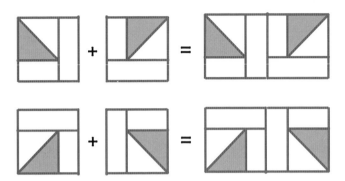

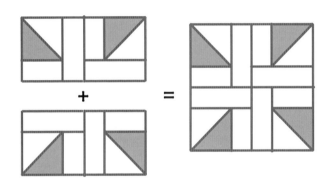

6. Select (2) 1½" x 10½" strips. Stitch to left and right sides of step 5 unit. Press seam toward the strips.

7. Select (2) 1½" x 12½" strips. Stitch to top and bottom of step 6 unit to complete one sashed Pinwheel block. Press seam toward the strips.

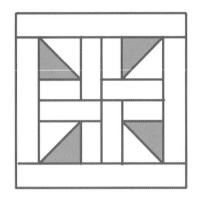

8. Repeat steps 1-7 to make (16) sashed Pinwheels blocks.

9. Lay out quilt with (4) blocks across and (4) blocks down. Alternate the position of the 1½" x 12½" strips every other block to continue the "woven" effect at the intersections.

10. Stitch block to block to form rows.

11. Stitch row to row to complete the quilt.

12. Layer backing, batting and quilt top. Quilt as desired.

13. Make binding by connecting 2½" strips end-to-end with diagonal seams until the length is 12" longer than the distance around the quilt top. Fold and press in half lengthwise for a double binding. Sew binding to quilt.

14. Make a label to identify this quilt as being your art and enjoy!

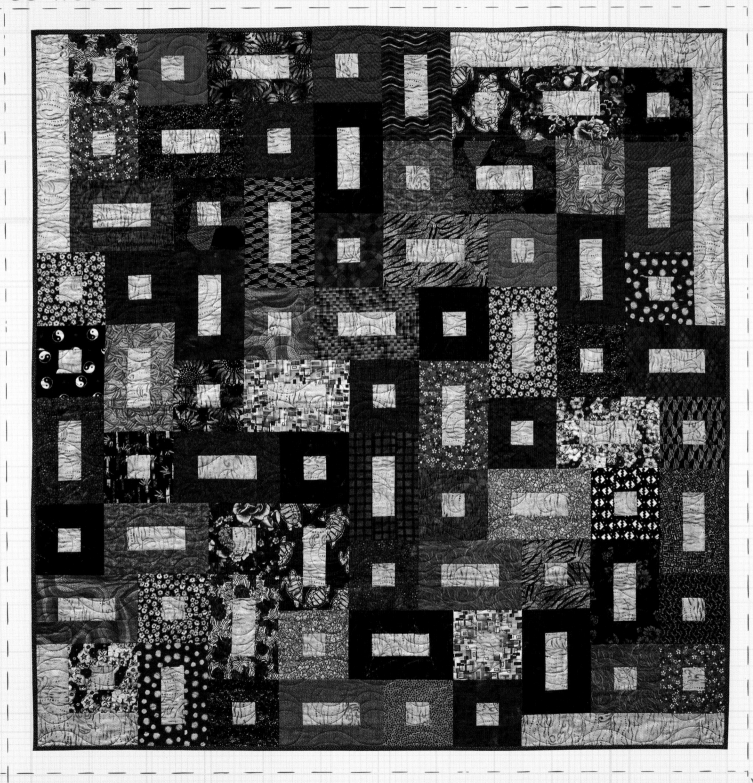

WEAVER

It's a puzzle...and the challenge is not in making the cobblestones or bricks, it's stitching the quilt together. Like the master basket weaver, you need to determine where to start and when to pause to get to the finish. In quilting, we mimic the basket weaver by doing partial seams. The bones of this design have dynamic movement and can be easily stylized to look modern or scrappy. Give it a try...embrace the partial seams as no big deal... become the master.

SUPPLIES

- (55) 2½" x 40" strips in assorted Choir fabric
- ½ yard for binding
- 1 yard Harmonizer fabric for center and border. Cut strips as needed.

STRIP LENGTH	QUANTITY
BRICKS 2½" X 24½"	34
COBBLESTONES 2½" X 18"	41

For Each Cobblestone

- From (1) 2½" Choir strip, crosscut (2) 2½" x 6½" and (2) 2½" x 2½" segments.
- From the Harmonizer, cut 2½" strip, crosscut (1) 2½" x 2½" segment.

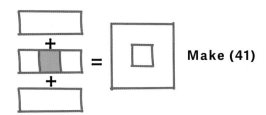

Make (41)

For Each Brick

- From (1) 2½" Choir strip, crosscut (2) 2½" x 6½" and (2) 2½" x 2½" segments.
- From the Harmonizer, cut 2½" strip, crosscut (1) 2½" x 5½" segment.

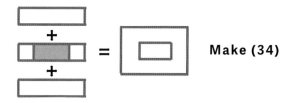

Make (34)

For the Border

- From the Harmonizer, cut 3½" strips, crosscut (1) 3½" x 6½", (1) 3½" x 9½"; (1) 3½" x 21½"; (1) 3½" x 24½", and (2) 3½" x 18½" segments.

INSTRUCTIONS

1. Make (41) Cobblestones.

2. Make (34) Bricks.

3. Stitch (1) Cobblestone to (1) Brick. Press seam. Make (28).

4. Lay out (7) Unit A and (7) Unit B configurations as follows. Stitch the Cobblestone/Brick units together lengthwise. Press seams.

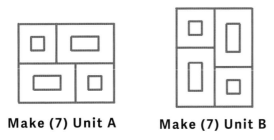

Make (7) Unit A   **Make (7) Unit B**

5. Lay out the entire **Weaver** design using Unit A and Unit B following the diagram for placement. Add the remaining Bricks and Cobblestones. (Omit the border sections.)

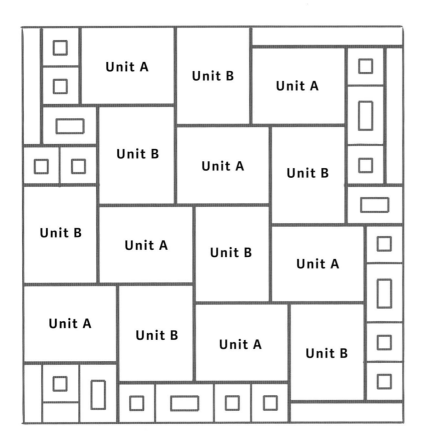

It's a Puzzle

NOTE: Sections are highlighted in the diagram. ** Denotes partial seam placement.

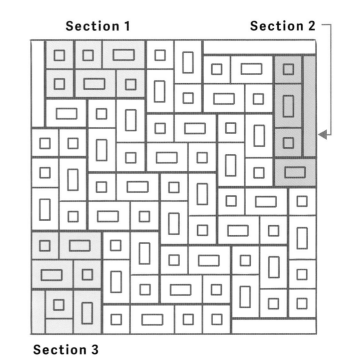

Section 1   Section 2

Section 3

SECTION 1

6. Stitch (2) Cobblestones together. Press seam. Then stitch to the end of (1) Unit A. Press seam.

SECTION 2

7. Stitch (1) Cobblestone to each end of (1) Brick. Then stitch to 3½" x 18½" border lengthwise. Press seam to the border. Add (1) Brick to the end. Press seam.

SECTION 3

8. Stitch (1) Cobblestone to 3½" x 6½" border, press seam to the border. Then stitch 3½" x 9½" border to the left side and (1) Brick to the right side. Press seams.

9. Stitch step 8 assembly to the bottom of Unit A.

13. Stitch (1) Cobblestone to one end and (2) Cobblestones to the other end of (1) Brick. Press seams. Then add to the right side of Unit A/B, lengthwise.

14. Add 3½" x 18½" border to bottom of section. Press seam to border.

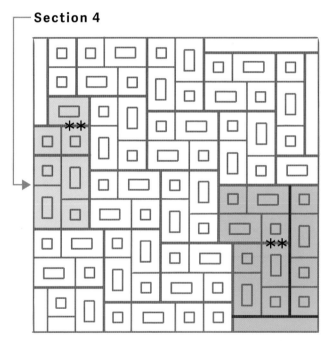

Section 4

Section 5

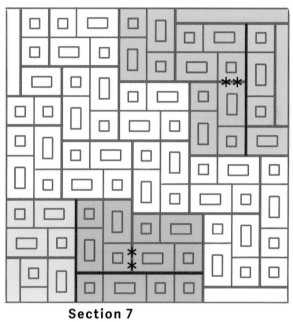

Section 6

Section 7

SECTION 4

10. Stitch (2) Cobblestones together. Press seam, then stitch to the top of (1) Unit B. Press seam.

11. Then stitch (1) Brick with a PARTIAL seam (**) to the top right side.

SECTION 5

12. Stitch Unit A and Unit B together on the right side with a PARTIAL seam (**).

SECTION 6

15. Stitch Unit A and Unit B together on the right side with a PARTIAL seam (**).

16. Stitch Section 2 to the right side, lengthwise. Press seam. Then add 3½" x 24½" border to the top of the assembly. Press seam toward the border.

17. Stitch Unit B to the top left of assembly. Press seam.

SECTION 7

18. Stitch Unit B and Unit A together at the bottom with a PARTIAL seam (**).

19. Stitch (1) Cobblestone to one end and (2) Cobble-stones to the other end of (1) Brick. Press seams. Then add to the bottom of Unit B/A, lengthwise.

20. Add Section 3 to the left side. Press seam.

Section 9

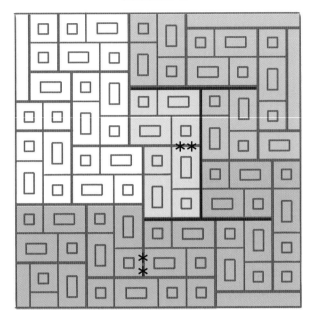

Section 8

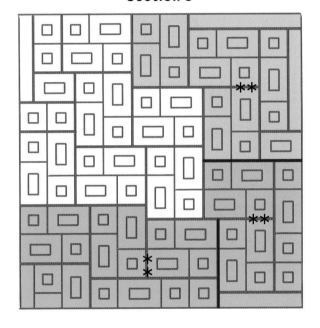

SECTION 9

23. Stitch Unit A and Unit B together on the right side with a PARTIAL seam (**).

24. Stitch the Unit A/B to the left center of Section 8. Press seam. Then complete the partial seam from Section 6 and the partial seam from Section 5. Press seams.

SECTION 8

21. Stitch Sections 5 and 6 together to join. Press seam.

22. Stitch Section 7 to Section 5 to join. Press seam.

Section 10

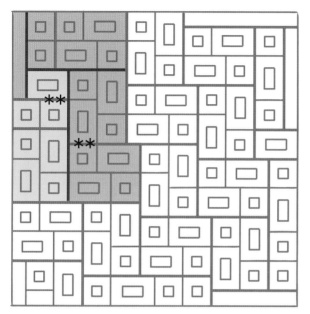

Final Assembly

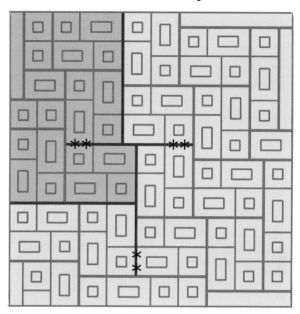

SECTION 10

25. Stitch Unit B and Unit A together on the left side with a PARTIAL seam (**).

26. Then stitch lengthwise to the right side of Section 4. Press seam.

27. Stitch Section 1 to the top of the assembly. Press seam. Then stitch (1) 3½" x 18" border to the left side. Press seam to the border.

28. Now complete the partial seam from Section 4. Press seam.

FINAL ASSEMBLY

29. Stitch Sections 9 and 10 to the top right seam between the sections. Press seam.

30. Stitch the bottom left seam between the sections. Press seam.

31. Then complete the bottom partial seam between the sections. And finally complete the partial seam across the center. Press seam.

Congratulations! You are now a master weaver.

32. Layer backing, batting and quilt top. Quilt as desired.

33. Make binding by connecting 2½" strips end-to-end with diagonal seams until the length is 12" longer than the distance around the quilt top. Fold and press in half lengthwise for a double binding. Sew binding to quilt.

34. Make a label to identify this quilt as being your art and enjoy!

MADE BY GYLEEN X FITZGERALD   QUILTED BY ASHLEY MALINOWSKI

SCRAPPY COBBLESTONES

USE IT UP!

The Cobblestone is an easy basic block. There are essentially no seams to match and it only takes two fabrics per block. To make it a "use it up" scrap quilt, collect 2½" x 20" strips for the Choir and pick one Harmonizer to pull it all together. I used every fabric that was "hanging around" my studio. What's in your stash just waiting to be used up?

SUPPLIES

- (100) 2½" X 20" strips of assorted Choir fabrics for Cobblestones
- 1½" yards Harmonizer fabric for center squares and border.
- 1 yard fabric for binding.

For Each Cobblestone

- From (1) 2½" Choir strip, crosscut (2) 2½" x 6½" and (2) 2½" X 2½" segments.
- Cut (1) 2½" X 40" Harmonizer strip*, crosscut (1) 2½" X 2½" square

Cut more as needed.

INSTRUCTIONS

1. Make 100 Cobblestones.

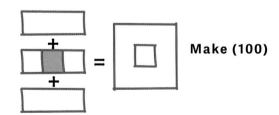

Make (100)

2. Lay out the quilt body (10 blocks X 10 blocks). Rotate every other Cobblestone to sew across seams.

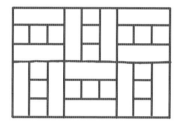

3. Stitch together block to block to form rows. Then stitch row to row to complete the quilt body. Press seams toward the 2½" X 6½" strips.

4. For the border, cut (8) 3" X 40" Harmonizer strips and stitch end to end.

5. Measure quilt from top to bottom; crosscut (2) strips to this length and stitch to the sides of the quilt. Press seams toward border.

6. Measure quilt from side to side; crosscut (2) strips to this length and stitch to top and bottom of quilt. Press seams toward border.

7. Layer backing, batting and quilt top. Quilt as desired.

   I really think machine quilting is the way to go for this highly graphic lap quilt. Select an overall edge to edge design. The sample is a 4" grid of spiraling squares.

8. Make binding by connecting (8) 2½" x 40" strips end-to-end using a diagonal seam. Fold and press in half lengthwise. Sew binding to quilt.

9. Make a label to identify this quilt as being your art and enjoy.

CAUGHT IN THE NET

To achieve a "border" look, you need to establish a clear definition between your border Cobblestones (light) and body Cobblestones (dark). I love how the center squares appear to just float across the quilt. **Caught in the Net** was machine quilted using a 30-degree grid, every 4".

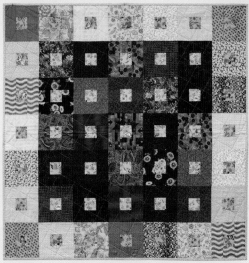

SUPPLIES

- ½ Yard—Soloist fabric bright or bold for center squares.

- (13) 2½" X 40" different dark Choir fabrics strips for body Cobblestones.

- (12) 2½" X 40" different light Choir strips for border Cobblestones.

For Cobblestones

- **CHOIR:** From each 2½" X 40" strip crosscut (6) 2½" X 6½".

- **SOLOIST:** Cut (5) 2½" X 40" strips. Crosscut (25) 2½" X 6½".

Make a set (makes 2 blocks): (6) 2½" X 6½" body or border (rectangle A) and (1) 2½" X 6½" Soloist (rectangle B). Pin these together. Make (13) dark sets and (12) light sets. Work one set at a time.

INSTRUCTIONS

1. Sew (1) rectangle A to each side of rectangle B.

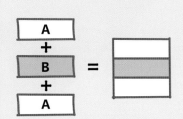

2. Crosscut at 2½". Cut (2).

3. Sew (1) rectangle A to each side of step 2. Make (2) Cobblestones.

You now have two completed Cobblestones or one set.

4. Repeat steps 1-3 to make (26) dark body Cobblestones and (24) light border Cobblestones.

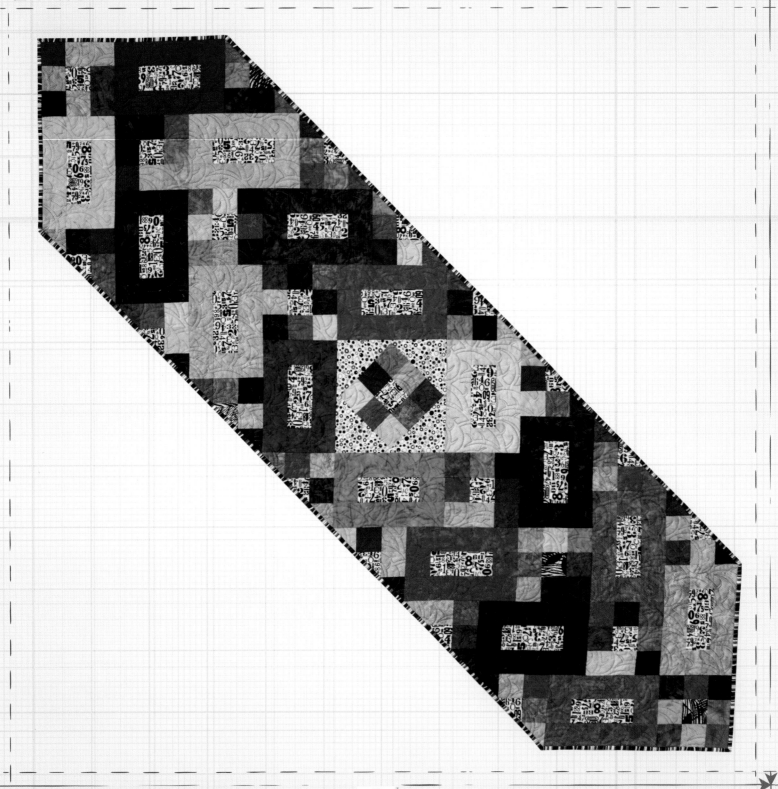

BUST THOSE SCRAPS!

BRILLIANT

Inspiration for building a quilt design can be right outside your back door. From a backyard patio, bricks and gravel came together in a crisscross pattern that became the bones for **Brilliant**. Designed to bust your scraps! Turning this table/bed runner into a bed quilt is just a matter of making more panels. What do you say when a good idea becomes great? Brilliant!

SUPPLIES

- (20) 2½" x 40" strips, assorted Choir fabrics. Crosscut (16) 2½" x 25" strips.
- 1 yard Harmonizer fabric
- Angle Trim Tool

COMPONENT	SIZE	QUANTITY
BRICKS	2½" X 25"	**16** (CHOIR)
	2½" X 5½"	**16** (HARMONIZER)
GRAVEL	2½" X 2½"	**142** (CHOIR)
		23 (HARMONIZER)

For Each Brick

- From (1) 2½" x 25" Choir strip, crosscut (2) 2½" x 9½" and (2) 2½" x 2½" segments.
- From the Harmonizer fabric cut 2½" strips, crosscut (1) 2½" x 5½" segment.

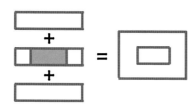

For 9-Patches and Pieced Half-Square Triangles

- From the remaining 2½" Choir strips, crosscut (142) 2½" x 2½" Gravel squares.
- From the 2½" Harmonizer fabric strips, crosscut for (23) 2½" x 2½" Gravel squares.

INSTRUCTIONS

1. Make (16) Bricks.

2. Using (8) 2½" Choir Gravel and (1) 2½" Harmonizer Gravel, lay out a 9-Patch block with the Harmonizer Gravel in the center.

3. Stitch square to square to form rows. Then row to row to complete the 9-Patch.

4. Make (9) 9-Patch blocks.

5. Using (5) 2½" Choir Gravel and (1) 2½" Harmonizer Gravel, lay out Pieced Triangle following the sketch. Note position of Harmonizer Gravel.

6. Stitch square to square. Then row to row with 3, 2, 1 squares in each row. Trim with Angle Trim Tool aligning seam lines with the lines on the tool. Discard trimmings!

7. Make (14) Pieced Triangles.

8. Using the Harmonizer fabric, cut (2) 5¾" x 5¾" squares. Crosscut on the diagonal for (4) Triangles.

9. Center and pin the long side of a Triangle to (1) pieced 9-Patch; stitch. Press seam toward the Triangle. Repeat to stitch the remaining (3) Triangles to the pieced 9-Patch.

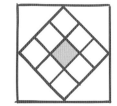

10. Trim assembly to 9½" x 9½" square to complete the center.

11. Stitch (1) Brick to the right side of the center. Press seam towards the Brick.

12. Stitch (1) Brick to (1) 9-Patch. Press seam towards the Brick.

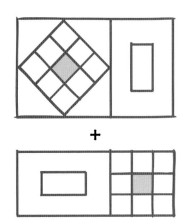

13. Stitch step 12 assembly to bottom of step 11. Press seam towards Step 12.

14. Stitch (1) Brick to (1) Pieced Triangle following the sketch. Press seam towards the Brick. Make (3), Unit A.

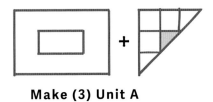

Make (3) Unit A

15. Stitch (1) Pieced Triangle to (1) Brick to (1) 9-Patch following sketch. Press seam towards the Brick. Make (3), Unit B.

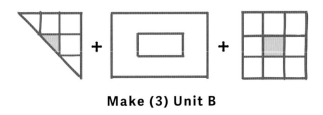

Make (3) Unit B

16. Stitch (1) Unit A to the right side of Step 13. Then stitch (1) Unit B to the bottom of the assembly.

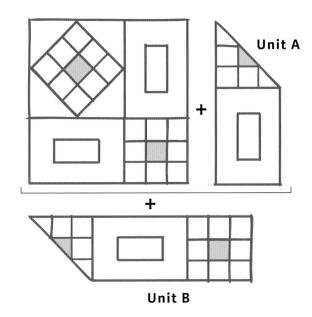

Unit A

Unit B

17. Continue adding Unit A to the right and Unit B to the bottom of the assembly to complete the bottom half of the table/bed runner.

18. Stitch (1) Pieced Triangle to (1) Brick following the sketch. Press seam towards the Brick. Make (4) Unit C.

Make (4) Unit C

19. Stitch (1) 9-Patch to (1) Brick to (1) Pieced Triangle following the sketch. Press seam towards the Brick. Make (4) Unit D.

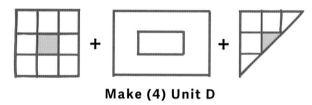

Make (4) Unit D

20. Stitch (1) Unit C to the top of assembly. Then stitch (1) Unit D to the left of assembly.

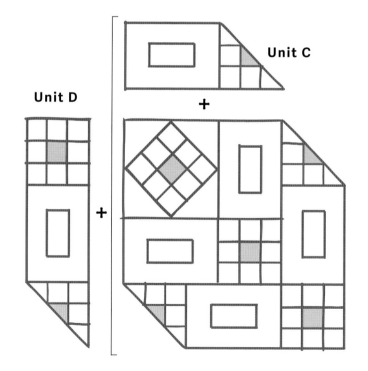

Unit C

Unit D

21. Continue adding Unit C to the top then Unit D to the left of the assembly to complete the top half of the table/bed runner.

22. Layer backing, batting and quilt top. Quilt as desired.

23. Make binding by connecting 2½" strips end-to-end with diagonal seams until the length is 12" longer than the distance around the quilt top. Fold and press in half lengthwise for a double binding. Sew binding to quilt.

24. Make a label to identify this quilt as being your art! Add a hanging sleeve if you plan to hang the quilt. Enjoy.

SQUARE TURN

I love illusions. Blink! You'll see hidden dimensions and shadows of elements appear. Architects are masters at creating these mind-bending impressions. Like the play between roof lines that appear to disappear as the sun takes it course. It works because of the flat plane; what we see while standing still. In that spirit, behold, the flat plane illusion of **Square Turn**. What do you see? Blink! It's your turn.

SUPPLIES

- (47) 2½" x 40" strips from (10-12) assorted Bright/Dark fabrics
- ¾ yard Bright/Dark Accent fabric for segments and binding

- (12) 2½" x 40" strips from (6-8) assorted Neutral/Light fabrics
- ⅔ yard Neutral/Light Accent fabric for segments and border
- Angle Trim Tool

COMPONENTS	BRIGHT/DARK	NEUTRAL/LIGHT
BRICKS	24	
COBBLESTONES	29	8
HALF-COBBLESTONES	16	16

For Two Half-Cobblestones

- From 2½" strip, crosscut (2) 2½" x 9½" and (2) 2½" x 2½" segments.
- From Accent fabric, cut 2½" strip. Crosscut (1) 2½" x 5½" segment.
- Using the Angle Trim Tool, trim twice to make (2) Half-Cobblestones.

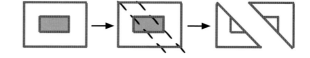

For Each Cobblestone

- From 2½" strip, crosscut (2) 2½" x 6½" and (2) 2½" x 2½" segments.
- From Accent fabric, cut 2½" strip. Crosscut (1) 2½" x 2½" square.

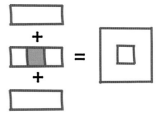

For Each Brick

- From (1) 2½" strip, crosscut (2) 2½" x 9½" and (2) 2½" x 2½" segments.
- From Accent fabric, cut 2½" strip. Crosscut (1) 2½" x 5½" segment.

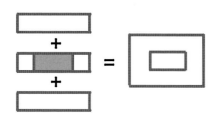

INSTRUCTIONS

1. Make (13) Cobblestones and (8) Bricks using the Bright/Dark strips and Accent fabric.

2. Using (9) Cobblestones, stitch Cobblestones to form a 9-Patch following sketch.

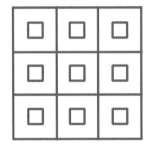

3. Using (8) Bricks, stitch together into pairs on the short side. Make (4) Brick pairs.

4. Stitch one Brick pair to left and right side of the 9-patch. Press seams toward the Brick pairs.

5. Stitch one Cobblestone to each end of the two remaining Brick pairs.

6. Stitch to the top and bottom of the 9-Patch assembly to complete the center. Press seam toward the Brick pairs.

7. Using border fabric, cut (2) 3½" x 30½" and (2) 3½" x 36½" strips.

8. Stitch the 3½" x 30½" border strips to the sides of the center. Press seams toward the borders.

9. Stitch the 3½" x 36½" border strips to the top and bottom of the center. Press seams toward the borders.

10. Make (16) Bright/Dark and (16) Neutral/Light Half-Cobblestones.

11. Stitch one Bright/Dark Half-Cobblestone to one Neutral/Light Half-Cobblestone. Make (16) Split-Cobblestones.

12. Make (4) Bricks and (4) Cobblestones using the Bright/Dark strips and Accent fabric.

13. Make (2) Cobblestones using the Neutral/Light strips and Accent fabric.

14. Using (4) Split-Cobblestones and (4) Bricks and (6) Cobblestones (from step 12 and 13), lay out two rows of components.

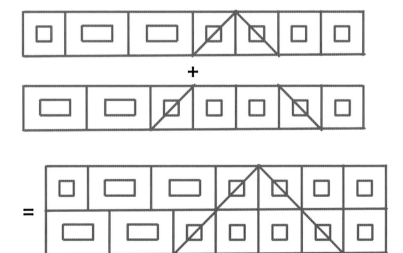

15. Stitch components to form rows, then row to row to complete the pieced border, Unit A.

16. Repeat steps 12-15. Make (4) pieced border Units: A1, A2, A3, A4.

17. Lay out pieced border Unit As with bordered center.

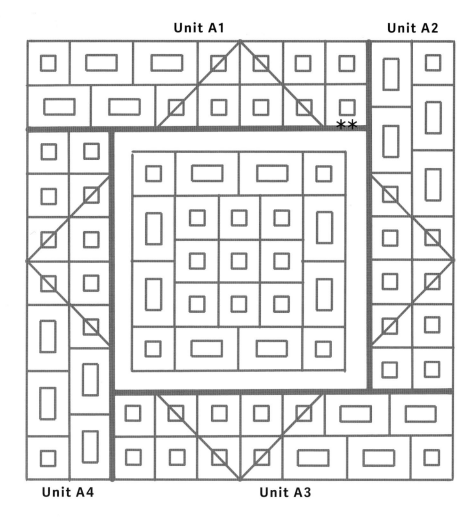

Unit A1

Unit A2

**

Unit A4

Unit A3

18. Stitch Unit A1 to bordered center partial seam (**). Stitch together for about 4". This forms the beginning of the partial seam.

19. Stitch Unit A2 to bordered center. This seam will include the end of the Unit A1 and the entire length of the bordered center.

20. Continue clockwise stitching Unit A3 and Unit A4 to the bordered center.

21. Now complete the partial seam of Unit A1.

22. Layer backing, batting and quilt top. Quilt as desired.

23. Using the binding fabric cut (6-7) 2½" x 40" strips. Make binding by connecting 2½" strips end-to-end with diagonal seams until the length is 12" longer than the distance around the quilt top. Fold and press in half lengthwise for a double binding. Sew binding to quilt.

24. Make a label to identify this quilt as being your art and attach a sleeve for hanging. Enjoy.

I'VE GOT THIS

A dynamo quilt that was inspired by the "I" patio paver pattern. I made two; one from self-made 2½" strips and one from pre-cut 2½" strips. The key to color and balance is to use a Harmonizer. Give it a try...embrace the partial seams as no big deal.

SUPPLIES

- (40) 2½" x 42" strips from assorted Choir fabrics.
- 1 yard Harmonizer fabric for center and sashing. Cut 2½" strips as needed.
- ½ yard for binding.

> **GOOD TO KNOW**
>
> Bricks take 2½" x 24" and you will make (30).
>
> Cobblestones take 2½" x 18" and you will make (36).

For Each Brick

- From 2½" Choir strips, cross cut (2) 2½" x 9½" and (2) 2½" x 2½" segments.
- From the Harmonizer, 2½" strip, cross cut (1) 2½" x 5½" segment.

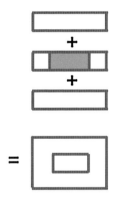

For Each Cobblestone

- From 2½" Choir strips, cross cut (2) 2½" x 9½" and (2) 2½" x 2½" segments.
- From the Harmonizer, 2½" strip, cross cut (1) 2½" x 5½" segment.

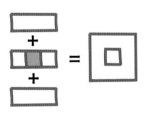

INSTRUCTIONS

1. Make (3) Cobblestones.

2. Make (2) Bricks.

3. Lay out (3) Cobblestones and (2) Bricks, Unit A.

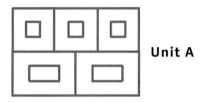

Unit A

4. Stitch the (3) Cobblestones together. To avoid matching seams, turn the center Cobblestone as shown. Press seam away from the center Cobblestone.

5. Stitch the (2) Bricks together. Do not worry about matching the seams block-to-block.

6. Stitch the two sections together. Press seam open or to either side.

7. Repeat steps 1-6 to make (3) Units: A1, A2 and A3.

8. Make (2) Cobblestones and (1) Brick. For Unit B, stitch the Cobblestones to the Brick using a partial seam (**). Begin at the outside edge and stitch two-thirds of the Cobblestone distance. Press seams toward the Brick.

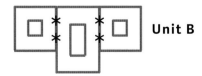

Unit B

9. To assemble the first half of the quilt; lay out the (4) Units A1, A2, A3 and B.

10. Stitch the straight edge of the Unit B to Unit A2. Press seam open or to one side.

11. Stitch Unit A1 and A3 to each side of the A2/B Unit. Press seam open or to one side.

12. For the second half of the quilt, repeat steps 1-11.

13. Make (4) Bricks. Stitch (2) together, end-to-end. Then repeat with the remaining (2) Bricks, Units C1 and C2.

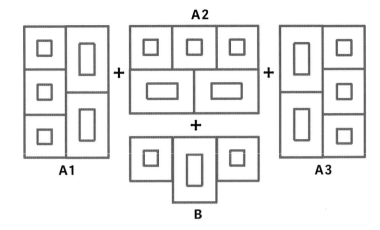

Unit C

14. Fold and pin the center partially stitched Bricks of Unit B onto itself. Stitch Unit C1 to left side of the 1st half of the quilt. Repeat for the right side using Unit C2. Press seam open or to one side.

15. Repeat step 14 for the 2nd half of the quilt.

16. Unpin the center Bricks of Unit B and stitch Bricks together end-to-end. Press seam open or to one side.

17. Complete the partial seams on both sides of the center Bricks. Press seams.

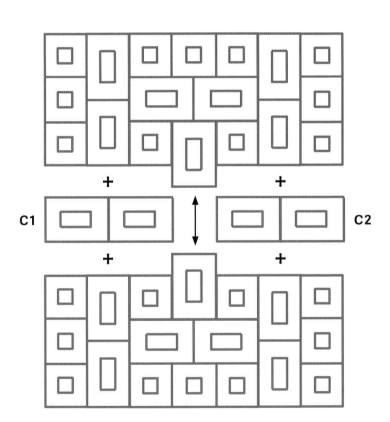

Border assembly

18. Make (14) Cobblestones and (12) Bricks.

19. Lay out each border side (1, 2, 3, 4). Place one Cobblestone block on each corner. Complete the border layout using the following (you decide on the order):

   • **Side 1 and Side 2:** (4) Cobblestones and (2) Bricks.

   • **Side 3 and Side 4:** (1) Cobblestone and (4) Bricks.

20. Stitch blocks end-to-end to complete each border strip (do not stitch the corner cobblestones).

21. Using the Harmonizer sashing fabric, cut (6) 2½" x 40" strips. Connect (5) strips end-to-end; then crosscut (4) 2½" x 42½". Using the remaining strips, cut (8) 2½" x 6½". Cut (4) 2½" x 2½" squares from any scrap remaining from the Choir strips.

22. Stitch (1) 2½" x 42½" sashing strip to left and right side of the quilt. Press seam towards the sashing.

23. Select (2) side borders. Stitch one to the left and one to the right of the quilt's sashing. Press seam towards the sashing.

24. Using the sashing segments, stitch (2) 6½" strips to the (2) 2½" squares to the 42½" strip as follows. Make (2). Stitch to top and bottom of quilt. Press seam towards the sashing.

25. To complete the top and bottom borders, stitch the corner Cobblestone to 6½" sashing to pieced border side to the 6½" sashing to the corner Cobblestone. Make (2).

26. Stitch to top and bottom of quilt. Press seams to the sashing.

27. Layer backing, batting and quilt top. Baste layers together. Quilt as desired.

28. From the ½ yd binding fabric, cut (6) 2½" strips. Connect the strips end-to-end using diagonal seams. Fold and press in half lengthwise for a double binding. Bind the edges of the quilt.

29. Add a label and make a sleeve (optional).

INNER CITY

From brownstones to row homes, the grid of a city is the same. City architects used a basic formula for the exterior dimensions; adding walls for functionality, then giving the neighborhoods character with the facades. That was my thinking for the bones of Inner City. Make the project table runner or pick from the matrix and make it your own.

SUPPLIES TABLERUNNER, UNITS A, C, D, and E

- (20) 2½" x 40" strips, assorted solids
- (38) 3½" x 3½" Pebbles, assorted fabric
- 1 yard binding fabric
- (6) 18" x 22" assorted fabrics for backing

UNIT	A	B	C	D	E	F
BRICKS	3	4	2	3	3	3
COBBLESTONES	2	0	4	1	2	1
3½" PEBBLES	9	11	7	13	7	9

NOTE: Units measure 21" W x 15" L

For Each Brick

- From (1) 2½" strip, crosscut (2) 2½" x 9½" and (2) 2½" x 2½" segments.
- From another 2½" strip, crosscut (1) 2½" x 5½" segment.

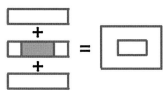

For Each Cobblestone

- From (1) 2½" strip, crosscut (2) 2½" x 6½" and (2) 2½" x 2½" segments.
- From another 2½" strip, crosscut (1) 2½" x 2½" square.

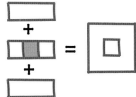

INSTRUCTIONS

1. Make (11) Bricks and (9) Cobblestones.

2. Lay out and stitch each Unit A, C, D and E following the sketch.

Unit A

BRICKS	3
COBBLESTONES	2
3½" PEBBLES	9

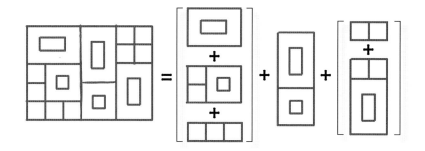

Unit B

BRICKS	4
COBBLESTONES	0
3½" PEBBLES	11

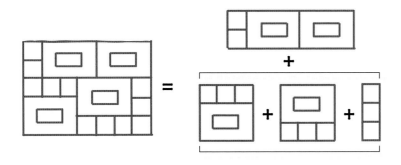

Unit D

BRICKS	3
COBBLESTONES	1
3½" PEBBLES	13

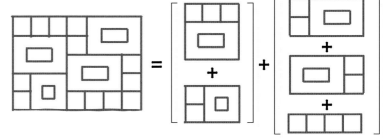

Unit C

BRICKS	2
COBBLESTONES	4
3½" PEBBLES	7

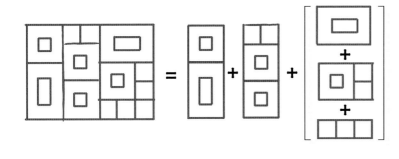

Unit E

BRICKS	3
COBBLESTONES	2
3½" PEBBLES	7

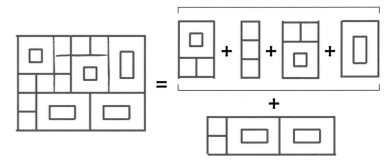

Unit F

BRICKS	3
COBBLESTONES	1
3½" PEBBLES	9

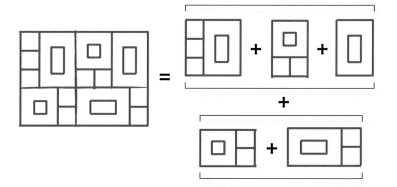

3. Assemble the table runner by stitching Units A to C to D to E together lengthwise.

4. Layer backing, batting and quilt top. Quilt as desired.

5. Make binding by connecting 2½" strips end-to-end with diagonal seams until the length is 12" longer than the distance around the quilt top. Fold and press in half lengthwise for a double binding. Sew binding to quilt.

6. Make a label or just initial this quilt as being your art.

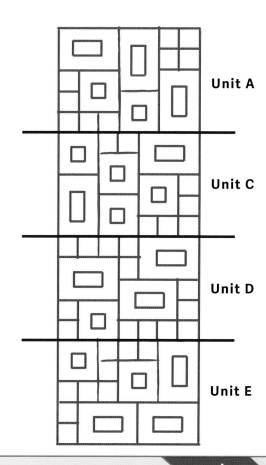

Unit A

Unit C

Unit D

Unit E

TIPS

To create a unique table runner, remember you can:

- Switch the order of the units

- Switch the order of the segments within the unit

- Reverse the unit or segment

- Select any (4) units as desired

- Re-purpose the table runner for a burst of color on a narrow wall

BONUS

Turn **Inner City** into a wall-hanging, lap or bed quilt by adding units and building columns.

A	F	E	D
B	A	F	E
C	B	A	F
D	C	B	A
E	D	C	B
F	E	D	C

◄ **Wall Hanging** 42" x 45"

◄ **Lap Quilt** 63" x 75"

◄ **Bed Quilt** 84" x 90"

MODERN AND MODULAR – GRAFFITI

A NEW PERSPECTIVE

MADE BY GYLEEN X. FITZGERALD

QUILTED BY ASHLEY MALINOWSKI

SUPPLIES

- (6) 3½" x 20" strips in assorted Pinwheel accent fabric
- (1) 18" x 22" Pinwheel background fabric
- 18" x 22" white or light neutral fabric
- 18" x 22" black or dark neutral fabric
- 1 yard background fabric
- ⅓ yard binding fabric
- Angle Trim Tool

Cutting

- Using the background fabric, cut (5) 6½" x 40" strips. Crosscut (18) 6½" x 9½" segments.
- Using the light neutral, cut (27) 3½" x 3½" Pebbles
- Using the dark neutral, cut (27) 3½" x 3½" Pebbles

Pinwheels

- Using the 3½" x 20" accent fabric and the Angle Trim Tool, cut (12) sets of (4) Triangles.
- Using the 18" x 22" background fabric, cut 3½" strips. Crosscut using the Angle Trim Tool (48) Triangles.

INSTRUCTIONS

1. Using the Triangles, make (12) 6½" Pinwheels.

2. Replace the Cobblestones with Pinwheels in the Unit assembly, and replace the Bricks with 6½" x 9½" rectangles in the Unit assembly.

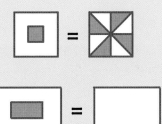

3. Stitch Units B and B (reverse); F and F (reverse); and C and C (reverse). Follow the sketch for the placement of the light and dark 3½" Pebbles.

4. Lay out Units following sketch. Stitch unit in pairs to make rows then row to row to complete the wall-hanging.

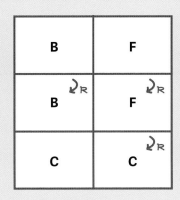

5. Layer backing, batting and quilt top. Quilt as desired.

6. Make binding by connecting 2½" strips end-to-end with diagonal seams until the length is 12" longer than the distance around the quilt top. Fold and press in half lengthwise for a double binding. Sew binding to quilt.

7. Make a label or just initial this quilt as being your art.

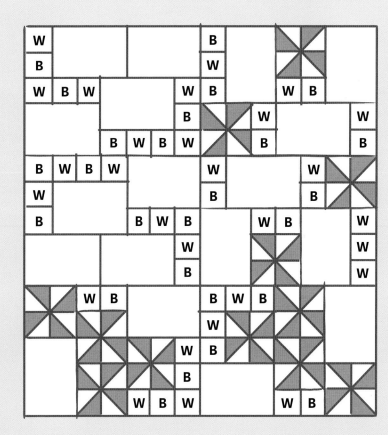

MADE BY MELANIE BARRETT   QUILTED BY JUDY M. CLARK

UPTOWN

Say "city" and I immediately think of Philly, the city of my youth. When you live in the city, coming of age is not about being old enough to drive a car… it's about being old enough to travel alone on the subway system. Boy, we thought we were grown with the whole world of New York City just a train ride away. Join me for the ride… we're going Uptown!

SUPPLIES

- (21) 2½" x 40" assorted light strips
- (21) 2½" x 40" assorted dark strips
- (60) 5" x 5" squares, assorted light (Fabric A) with at least (2) squares per fabric*
- (60) 5" x 5" squares, assorted dark (Fabric B) with at least (2) squares per fabric*
- ⅔ yards binding fabric

*NOTE: ½ yard (cut into (60) 5" squares) if using one fabric for light or dark.

INSTRUCTIONS

1. Select (2) 5" squares of (1) Fabric A and (2) 5" squares of (1) Fabric B. Mark a diagonal line on the wrong side of Fabric A. Pair together one light and one dark with right sides together. Stitch ¼" from BOTH sides of the diagonal line.

2. Cut apart on the diagonal line and press towards the dark triangle to make (4) Half-Square Triangles. Lay out (4) Half-Square Triangles as follows. Then stitch (2) together to form pairs. Finally, stitch pairs together to form a Pinwheel.

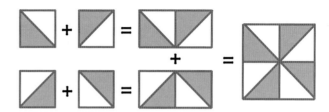

3. Trim the Pinwheel square to 8½" x 8½" unfinished.

4. Repeat steps 1-3 to make (30) Pinwheels.

5. Select (4) 2½" x 40" strips, (2) light and (2) dark. Crosscut each strip: (1) 2½" x 4½" short (S) and (1) 2½" x 6½" long (L).

6. Lay out the full block where the light segments are in the 1 and 3 positions and the dark segments are in the 2 and 4 positions.

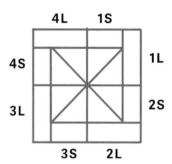

7. Stitch the following long segment and short segment together: 4L + 1S, 3L + 4S, 2L + 3S, and 1L + 2S. Press seams to the long segment.

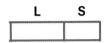

L   S

8. Stitch 4L + 1S to Pinwheel with a partial seam. Press seam toward the segment.

9. Going in a clockwise rotation, stitch 1L + 2S to the pinwheel unit. Then stitch the 2L + 3S followed by the 3L + 4S. Press seams toward the segment.

10. Complete the 4L + 1S partial seam. Press seam toward the segment.

11. Repeat steps 5-10 to make (30) blocks.

12. Lay out quilt with (5) blocks across and (6) blocks down.

13. Stitch block to block to form rows.

14. Stitch row to row to complete the quilt.

15. Layer backing, batting and quilt top. Quilt as desired.

16. Make binding by connecting 2½" strips end-to-end with diagonal seams until the length is 12" longer than the distance around the quilt top. Fold and press in half lengthwise for a double binding. Sew binding to quilt.

17. Make a label to identify this quilt as being your art and enjoy!

ICY

INSTRUCTIONS

COMPONENT	LIGHT	DARK
5" SQUARES	32*	32*
2½" X 40" STRIPS	11	11

*Two squares of each fabric.

SCRAPPY BORDER: Icy was made using three pre-cut fabric collections: one for the 2½" strips and two for the 5" charm squares. Since only sixteen blocks were made there were plenty of leftovers to make a pieced border. The strips were randomly cut to various lengths and sewn end to end. From there it's just a matter of using the pieced strip as border fabric. I added two borders. However, the strips didn't seem to end. Scrappy Binding! Done.

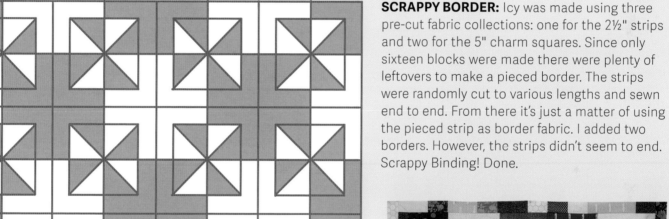

ALTERNATE LAYOUT

18" x 12"

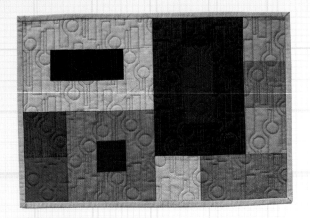

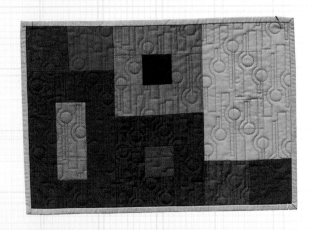

SMALL PLATES — QUILT TAPAS

Each placemat is 18" x 12" and uses a medley of solids. Using prints, however, would make these quick small plates appetizing as well. Feel free to rotate or change the order of the column. Each Tapas can be the same or as individualized as you like. Making four would be a perfect gift—a foodie's delight. Have fun and enjoy the sampling of Quilt Tapas.

SUPPLIES

- (8) 2½" x 40" strips in assorted fabrics for Bricks
- (14) 2½" x 22" strips in assorted fabrics for Cobblestones
- (40) 3½" x 3½" Pebbles in assorted fabrics
- 1 yard binding fabric
- (6) 18" x 22" assorted fabrics for backing

COMPONENT	QUANTITY
BRICKS	8
COBBLESTONES	14
3½" PEBBLES	40

For Each Brick

- From (1) 2½" strip, crosscut (2) 2½" x 9½" and (2) 2½" x 2½" segments.
- From another 2½" strip, crosscut (1) 2½" x 5½" segment.

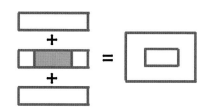

- Make (8) Bricks.

For Each Cobblestone

- From (1) 2½" strip, crosscut (2) 2½" x 6½" and (2) 2½" x 2½" segments
- From another 2½" strip, crosscut (1) 2½" x 2½" square.
- Make (14) Cobblestones.

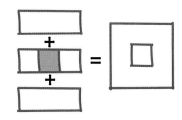

INSTRUCTIONS

1. Lay out and stitch each Small Plate following the sketches.

BRICKS	2
COBBLESTONE	1
3½" PEBBLES	8

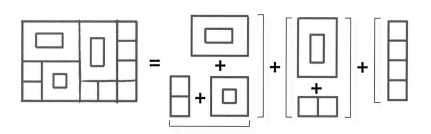

BRICKS	2
COBBLESTONES	2
3½" PEBBLES	4

BRICKS	1
COBBLESTONES	3
3½" PEBBLES	6

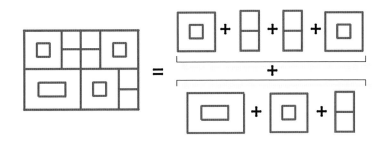

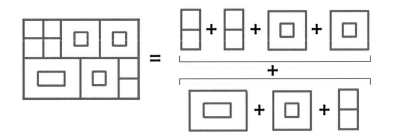

BRICKS	1
COBBLESTONES	3
3½" PEBBLES	6

BRICKS	1
COBBLESTONES	3
3½" PEBBLES	6

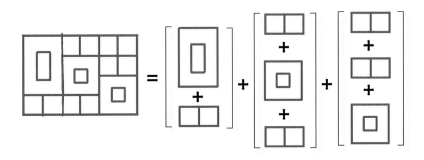

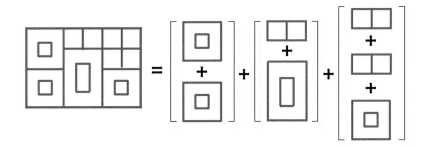

BRICKS	1
COBBLESTONES	2
3½" PEBBLES	10

2. Layer backing, batting and quilt top. Quilt as desired.

3. For each Small Plate's binding, connect (2) 2½" x 40" strips end-to-end with a diagonal seam. Fold and press in half lengthwise for a double binding. Sew binding to quilt.

4. Make a label or just initial each quilt as being your art. Bon Appetit.

GYLEEN'S ALMOST PERFECT BINDING

This is my classic binding technique. Making placemats is a great place to practice. This binding gets the job done without a lot of stress. Remember practice makes...almost perfect.

The binding will make or break a quilt. Yet, it is one of the hardest topics to explain in words. Regardless, here goes! Between the words and the sketches, I think you will understand the process.

1. Hand stitch (baste) around your completed quilt. This is the most tedious step in the process.

2. Cut the binding 2½" and connect needed strips end-to-end using diagonal seams. Press in half, lengthwise.

    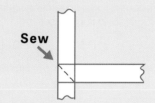

    Sew

3. Using a walking foot start stitching with ⅜" seam allowance about 8-10" from the upper right corner.

4. For the corner, stitch to the end of the side. Gently remove stitches until the binding is in line with the next edge of the quilt.

    Binding inline with quilt

    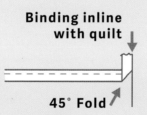

    45° Fold

5. Bring down the binding creating a fold that is even with the top edge you just stitched. Stitch this side of the quilt. Complete all remaining corners. Stop stitching when you are 8-10" from where you started.

    Fold even with quilt edge

6. Gently overlap the ends of the binding so they lay smooth. Make a ⅛" clip through all layers of the binding at the midway point of your unstitched edge. DON'T CLIP THE QUILT.

    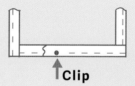

    ↑Clip

7. Open binding and overlap; the clips are the alignment markers. Mark then stitch on the 45-degree diagonal line. The ends of your binding should be on the same side of the marked line.

    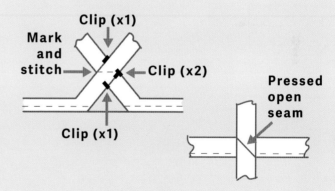

    Clip (x1)

    Mark and stitch

    Clip (x2)

    Clip (x1)

    Pressed open seam

8. Trim excess binding leaving ¼" seam allowance. Continue to sew binding to quilt.

9. Zig-zag around the quilt in the seam allowance. Trim quilt and discard batting and backing.

10. Turn binding to back. Finesse corners and hand-stitch fold to quilt. Done.

MADE BY GYLEEN X FITZGERALD   QUILTED BY ASHLEY MALINOWSKI

TRIO

It's old school wisdom that things or events happen in threes. I tend to find my design balance using a trio or a visual repeat of three. Hence, how Trio got its name. Three blocks: Bricks, Cobblestones, and Pinwheels. Three tones: light, bright and dark. Three columns and three rows. That's how this design game gets played. How do you play "Trio"?

SUPPLIES

- (7-8) Dark fabrics; cut (15) 2½" x 40" and (3) 3½" x 9" strips
- (7-8) Bright fabrics; cut (30) 2½" x 40" and (6) 3½" x 9" strips
- ½ yard Light fabric, cut 2½" and 3½" strips as needed
- ½ yard for binding
- Angle Trim tool

COMPONENT		QUANTITY
BRICKS	**12** (DARK)	**24** (BRIGHT)
COBBLESTONES	**6** (DARK)	**12** (BRIGHT)
6½" PINWHEELS	**3** (DARK)	**6** (BRIGHT)

For Each Brick

- From (1) 2½" Dark or Bright strip, crosscut (2) 2½" x 9½" and (2) 2½" x 2½" segments.
- From 2½" Light fabric, crosscut (1) 2½" x 5½" segment.

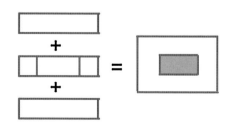

For Each Cobblestone

- From (1) 2½" Dark or Bright strip, crosscut (2) 6½" x 2½" and (2) 2½" x 2½" segments.
- From 2½" Light fabric, crosscut (1) 2½" x 2½" segment.

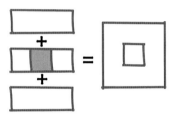

For Each Pinwheel

- From (1) 3½" x 9½" Dark or Bright strip, crosscut (4) Triangles using the Angle Trim tool.
- From 3½" Light fabric strips, crosscut (4) Triangles using the Angle Trim tool.

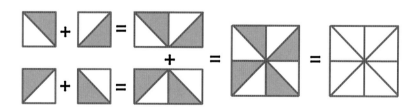

INSTRUCTIONS

1. Make (12) Dark Bricks.

2. Pair Bricks together and stitch on short side. Make (6) pairs, Unit A.

Make (6) Unit A

3. Make (6) Dark Cobblestones.

4. Make (3) Dark Pinwheels.

5. Stitch (2) Dark Cobblestones to a Pinwheel, one on each side. Make (3) Unit B.

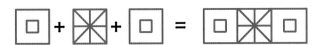

Make (3) Unit B

6. Stitch (2) Unit As to Unit B, one on each side.
   Make (3) Dark Blocks.

7. Repeat steps 1-6 using Bright and Light fabric. Make (6) Bright Blocks.

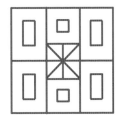

8. Lay out (3) Dark and (6) Bright Blocks (rotating the block to avoid matching seams).

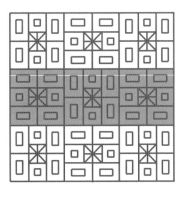

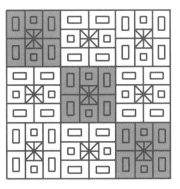
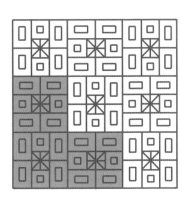

9. Stitch block to block to form rows. Then stitch row to row to complete the assembly of the quilt.

10. Layer backing, batting and quilt top. Quilt as desired.

11. Make binding by connecting 2½" strips end-to-end with diagonal seams until the length is 12" longer than the distance around the quilt top. Fold and press in half lengthwise for a double binding. Sew binding to quilt.

12. Make a label to identify this quilt as being your art and enjoy!

CITY HALL

Bright lights...big city. Cityscapes fascinate me. Some are so distinctive they can be identified solely by their silhouette. Looking out above the traffic on a starry night, I can see the buildings glow. Do they light the way to City Hall?

SUPPLIES

- (16) 2½" x 26" strips in assorted Choir fabric for Bricks
- (17) 2½" x 20" strips in assorted Choir fabric for Cobblestones
- (48) 3½" x 3½" Pebbles in assorted Choir fabric
- ⅔ yard Harmonizer fabric for centers and border
- ½ yard binding

COMPONENT	QUANTITY
BRICKS	16
COBBLESTONES	17
3½" PEBBLES	48

For Each Brick

- Using (16) strips, cut (2) 2½" x 9½" and (2) 2½" x 2½" segments from each strip.
- Using Harmonizer fabric cut (2-3) 2½" strips, crosscut (16) 2½" x 5½" segments.

For Each Cobblestone

- Using (17) strips, cut (2) 2½" x 6½" and (2) 2½" x 2½" from each strip.
- Using Harmonizer fabric cut (1) 2½" strip, crosscut (17) 2½" x 2½" square.

For border

- Using Harmonizer fabric, cut (4) 3½" strips; crosscut (4) 3½" x 15½", (2) 3½" x 12½", (4) 3½" x 9½" and (2) 3½" x 6½" segments.

INSTRUCTIONS

1. Make (16) Bricks.

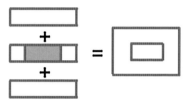

2. Make (17) Cobblestones.

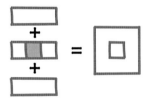

3. Pair 3½" Pebbles by twos for (24) pairs; sew together and press seam to one side.

4. Stitch (1) Pebble pair to the end of (16) Cobblestones.

5. Select (8) Pebble/Cobblestone units and stitch together in pairs along the Cobblestone edge. Make (4) Unit A.

Unit A

6. Stitch (1) Brick to each side of the remaining (8) Pebble/Cobblestone units. Make (8) Unit B.

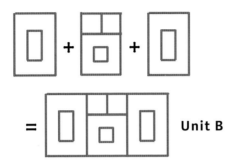

Unit B

7. Select (2) Unit Bs and (1) Unit A. Stitch the Unit B to each side of the Unit A. Make (4) Units: C1, C2, C3, C4.

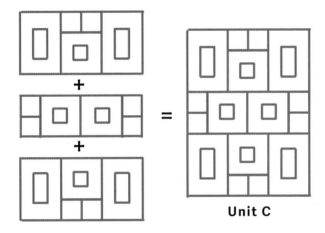

Unit C

8. Lay out the Unit Cs following the sketch for orientation. Place a Cobblestone in the center.

Unit C1 **Unit C4**

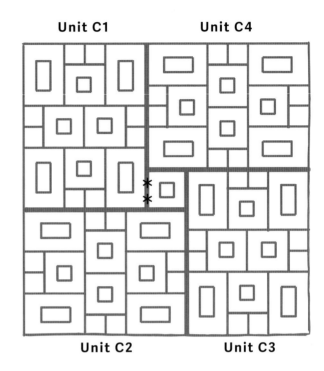

Unit C2 **Unit C3**

9. Start with a partial seam (**). Sew the center Cobblestone to Unit C1, stitch from the edge about 3". Press seam toward Unit C1.

10. Stitch Unit C2 across Unit C1/Cobblestone. Press seam toward Unit C2.

11. Stitch Unit C3 across Unit C2/Cobblestone. Press seam toward Unit C3.

12. Stitch Unit C4 across Unit C3/Cobblestone. Press seam toward Unit C4.

13. Now complete the partial seam between Unit C4 and Unit C1/Cobblestone.

14. For the side borders, stitch together 3½" x 9½", Pebble pair, 3½" x 15½", Pebble pair and 3½" x 6½". Make (2).

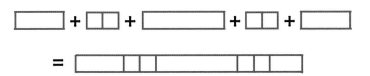

15. Stitch to left and right sides of the quilt. Press seams toward the borders.

16. For the top and bottom borders, stitch together 3½" x 12½", Pebble pair, 3½" x 15½", Pebble pair and 3½" x 9½". Make (2).

17. Stitch to top and bottom of quilt. Press seams toward the borders.

18. Make binding by connecting (5) 2½" x 40" strips end-to-end using diagonal seams. Fold and press in half lengthwise. Sew binding to quilt.

19. Make a label to identify this quilt as being your art and enjoy. Add a sleeve if desired.

BABY'S GOT BACK

BONUS

A gathering of yellows, leftover blues, a humming Harmonizer and one stunning Soloist are the building components to the baby's back!

COMPONENTS	SIZE	QTY.
BLOCKS	15" SQUARE	9
SASHING	6½" X 15"	12
CORNERSTONE	12½" X 12½"	1

Cornerstone Signature Block

- (12) 3½" pebbles
- (1) 6½" x 6½" square

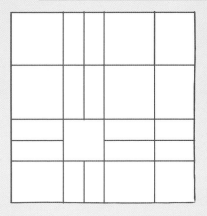

SO SQUARE - MODERN

When it comes to fabric, the idea of "modern" is played out in so many different directions that, rest assured, whatever fabric you choose to use, all will be wonderful. I used a collection of solids, about 15 of them. Semi-solids or batiks would give you that same clean-line look as well.

SUPPLIES

- (15-20) 6½" x 40" strips in assorted Choir fabric
- (15-20) 3½" x 22" strips in assorted Choir fabric
- 1 yard Harmonizer fabric for border and binding
- Angle Trim Tool

From (15-20) 6½" x 40" Choir strips

- Cut (18) 6½" x 9½" rectangles
- Cut (40) 6½" x 6½" squares
- Cut (20) 6½" Triangles using the Angle Trim Tool

From (15-20) 3½" x 22" Choir strips

- Cut (36) 3½" x 3½" squares

INSTRUCTIONS

Round A, Center

1. Pair 3½" squares by twos for (18) units; sew together and press seam to one side.

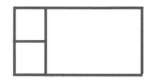

2. Sew (1) square unit to each 6½" x 9½" rectangle and press seam toward the rectangle. Make (18).

Make (18)

3. Sew together in the following configurations: Make (5) Unit A. Make (4) Unit B

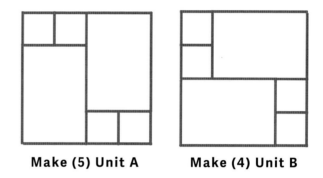

Make (5) Unit A   **Make (4) Unit B**

4. Lay out Units A and B in the following 9-Patch configuration:

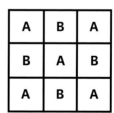

A	B	A
B	A	B
A	B	A

5. Stitch unit to unit for form rows. Then stitch row to row.

Round B, Border

6. Using the Harmonizer fabric, cut (4) 3¾" x 39¾" strips for the border. The most accurate way to do this is to cut the strips, then fold each strip in half. Measure from the fold to 20" and cut. Then trim ¼" off one end of a single layer. Repeat for each strip.

7. Using 1st strip of border, sew to Round A with a partial seam (**). Stitch together for about 4". Press seam toward the border. This forms the beginning of the partial seam.

8. Stitch the 2nd border strip to Round A, this seam will include the end of the first border strip and the entire length of Round A. Press seam toward the border.

9. Continue with the 3rd and 4th border strips. Press seams toward the borders.

10. Now complete the partial seam (**) of the 1st border strip. Press seam toward the border.

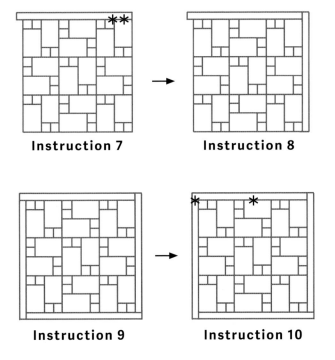

Instruction 7   **Instruction 8**

Instruction 9   **Instruction 10**

Round C, Corner

11. Divide the 6½" squares and 6½" Triangles into (4) groups. Each group will make (1) corner.

12. Lay out a corner per sketch. Sew together to form the rows; then stitch row to row.

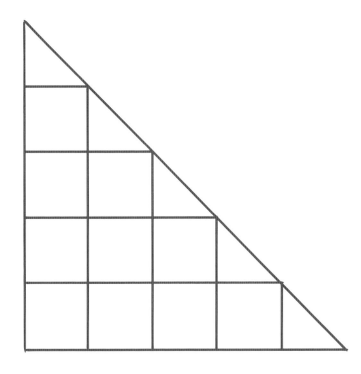

13. Repeat to make (4) corners.

14. Stitch one corner to each side of Round B. Pin, Pin, Pin. Press seams toward the border.

15. Layer backing, batting and quilt top. Quilt as desired.

16. Make binding by connecting 2½" strips end-to-end with diagonal seams until the length is 12" longer than the distance around the quilt top. Fold and press in half lengthwise for a double binding. Sew binding to quilt.

17. Make a label to identify this quilt as being your art and enjoy!

SO SQUARE – SCRAPPY

A CHANGE OF PERSPECTIVE... *Got 2½" strips and 2 yards of Soloist fabric?*

MADE BY
GYLEEN X. FITZGERALD

QUILTED BY
ASHLEY MALINOWSKI

SUPPLIES

- (40) 2½" x 40" assorted Choir strips
- 1 yard Harmonizer fabric
- 2 yard Soloist fabric

For **So Square– Scrappy** make or cut the following

BRICKS	28
COBBLESTONES	20
HALF-COBBLESTONES	20
3½" x 6½" RECTANGLES (SOLOISTS)	18

For Each Brick

- From 2½" Choir strip, crosscut (2) 2½" x 9½" and (2) 2½" x 2½" segments.
- From 2½" Harmonizer strip, crosscut (1) 2½" x 5½" segment
- Make (28) Bricks

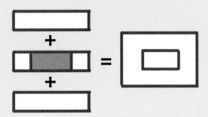

For Each Cobblestone

- From the 2½" Choir strip, crosscut (2) 2½" x 6½" and (2) 2½" x 2½" segments
- From the 2½" Harmonizer strip, crosscut (1) 2½" x 2½" square segment
- Make (20) Cobblestones

For (2) Half-Cobblestones

- Using a Brick, cut twice per sketch with the Angle Trim Tool to make (2) Half-Cobblestones

- Make (20) Half-Cobblestones

INSTRUCTIONS: Unless otherwise stated, follow instructions for **So Square — Modern**.

Round A, Center

1. Sew (1) 3½" x 6½" rectangle to (1) Brick. Press seam toward the rectangle. Make (18).

2. Sew together for Unit A and Unit B following the sketch: Make (5) Unit A. Make (4) Unit B

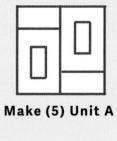

Make (5) Unit A

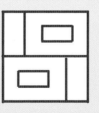

Make (4) Unit B

3. Lay out Units A and B in the following 9-Patch configuration:

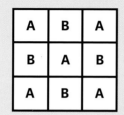

A	B	A
B	A	B
A	B	A

4. Stitch unit to unit forming rows. Then stitch row to row.

Round B, Border

5. Using Soloist fabric, cut (4) 3¾" x 39¾" strips for border. Follow steps 6-10 of **So Square — Modern** to cut and stitch border to Round A.

Round C, Corner

6. Divide the Cobblestones and Half-Cobblestones into (4) groups. Each group will make (1) corner.

7. Lay out a corner, see sketch. Sew together to form the rows. Then stitch row to row.

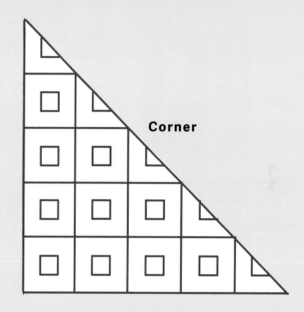

Corner

8. Repeat to make (4) corners.

9. Stitch one corner to each side of Round B. Pin, Pin, Pin. Press seams toward the sashing.

10. Layer backing, batting and quilt top. Quilt as desired.

11. Make binding by connecting 2½" strips end-to-end with diagonal seams until the length is 12" longer than the distance around the quilt top. Fold and press in half lengthwise for a double binding. Sew binding to quilt.

12. Make a label to identify this quilt as being your art and enjoy!

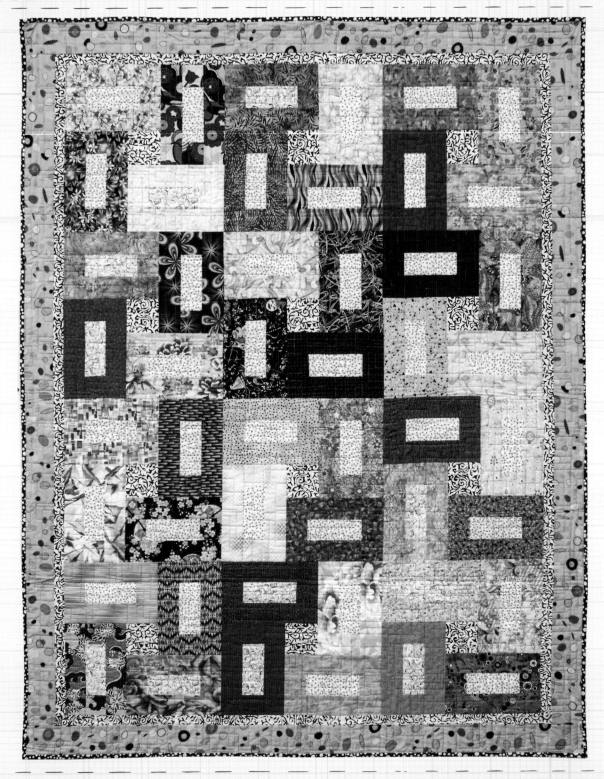

ZIP ZAP

What do you get when you elongate a Cobblestone block? The Brick. Zip Zap block takes the brick design one step further. Bricks frame a Pebble in-the-round using a partial seam. The blocks are large and quick to piece producing a lap quilt in a weekend. So, get out all those 2½" strips that you have been saving and put the zip in your zap!

SUPPLIES

- (50) 2½" x 25" strips, assorted Choir fabrics for Bricks
- 1 yard Harmonizer fabric for center strips, Pebbles and Border 1.
- 1 yard Soloist fabric for Border 2.
- 1 yard for binding.

For Each Brick

- From (1) 2½" Choir strip, crosscut (2) 2½" x 9½" and (2) 2½" x 2½" segments.
- From the Harmonizer fabric, cut (1) 2½" strip, crosscut (1) 2½" x 5½" segment.

For Each Zip Zap Block

- (1) 3½" x 3½" Pebble cut from the Harmonizer fabric
- (4) Bricks

INSTRUCTIONS

1. Make (4) Bricks.

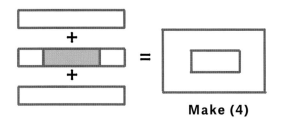

Make (4)

2. Lay out (4) Bricks and (1) 3½" Pebble, see sketch below.

3. Start with a partial seam (**) by sewing the 3½" Pebble to Brick 1, stitch only about 2". Press seam toward Brick 1.

4. Sew Brick 2 across the top of Brick 1 and Pebble. Press toward Brick 2. Sew Brick 3 across the top of Brick 2 and 3½" Pebble. Sew Brick 4 across the top of Brick 3 and 3½" Pebble.

5. Complete the partial seam (**) between Brick 4 and Brick 1.

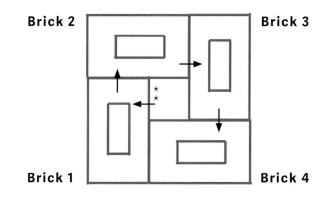

6. Repeat steps 1-5 to make a total of (12) Zip Zap blocks.

7. Layout the Zip Zap blocks (3) across and (4) down. Stitch together block to block to form rows. Then stitch row to row to complete the quilt center.

8. For Border 1, cut (6) 1½" x 40" strips and stitch end to end.

9. Measure quilt from top to bottom; crosscut (2) strips to this length. Stitch to the sides of the quilt. Press seams toward border.

10. Measure quilt from side to side; crosscut (2) strips to this length. Stitch to top and bottom of quilt. Press seams toward border.

11. For Border 2, cut (7) 3½" x 4" strips and stitch end to end.

12. Measure quilt from top to bottom; crosscut (2) strips to this length. Stitch to the sides of the quilt. Press seams toward border.

13. Measure quilt from side to side; crosscut (2) strips to this length. Stitch to top and bottom of quilt. Press seams toward border.

14. Layer backing, batting and quilt top. Quilt as desired. I really think machine quilting is the way to go for this highly graphic lap quilt. Select an overall edge to edge design.

15. Make binding by connecting (7) 2½" x 40" strips end-to-end using a diagonal seam. Fold and press in half lengthwise. Sew binding to quilt.

16. Make a label to identify this quilt as being your art and enjoy.

QUILT OF VALOR

This quilt was completed as part of a special project honoring the twelve remaining Tuskegee Airman who served in WWII living in the Washington DC metropolitan area. The 2½" strips for this Quilt of Valor were generously donated by members of the Bricks, Cobblestones and Pebbles Facebook group page. It is 4 blocks across and 5 blocks down, without a border, and finishes 60" x 75".

TOWN CENTER SQUARE

A CHANGE OF PERSPECTIVE

MADE BY
GYLEEN X. FITZGERALD

QUILTED BY
ASHLEY MALINOWSKI

SUPPLIES

- (40) 2½" x 25" strips, in assorted Choir fabrics

- 1 yard Soloist fabric

- ½ yard binding fabric

INSTRUCTIONS

Round A, Center

1. Follow steps 1-5 of Zip Zap pattern, page 91 to make a total of (4) Zip Zap blocks.

2. Lay out the Zip Zap blocks (2) across and (2) down. Stitch together block to block to form rows. Then stitch row to row to complete the quilt center.

Round B, Border

3. From the Soloist fabric, cut (2) 2½" x 30½" strips and (2) 2½" x 34½" strips for the border.

4. Using the (2) 2½" x 30½" strips, center and stitch to opposite sides of the quilt.

5. Using the (2) 2½" x 34½" strips, center and stitch to the remaining sides of the quilt.

Round C, Corners

6　From the Soloist fabric cut (8) 3½" x 6½" rectangles.

7. **For Each Brick**

   - From 2½" Choir strip, crosscut (2) 2½" x 9½" and (2) 2½" x 2½" segments.
   - From Soloist fabric, cut (1) 5½" x 2½" segment.
   - Make (16) Bricks.

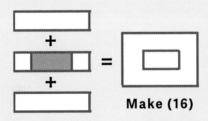

Make (16)

8. Crosscut (8) Bricks into Half-Cobblestones using the Angle Trim Tool.

9. **For Each Cobblestone**

   - From 2½" Choir strip, crosscut (2) 2½" x 6½" and (2) 2½" x 2½" segments.
   - From Harmonizer fabric, cut (1) 2½" x 2½" segment.
   - Make (8) Cobblestones.

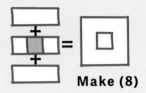

Make (8)

10. Using the Bricks, Cobblestones, Half-Cobblestones and rectangles, stitch corner Unit A together by rows, then row to row following sketch. Make (2).

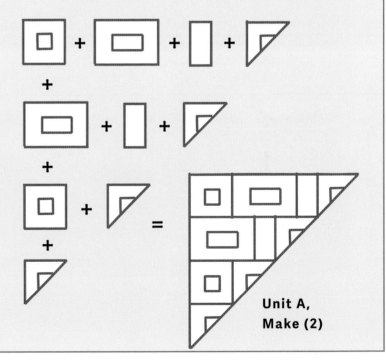

Unit A, Make (2)

11. Stitch Unit A to opposite sides of Round B.

12. Using the Bricks, Cobblestones, Half-Cobble-stones and rectangles, stitch corner Unit B together by rows. Then stitch row to row following sketch. Make (2).

13. Stitch Unit B to remaining sides of Round B.

14. Layer backing, batting and quilt top. Quilt as desired.

15. Make binding by connecting 2½" strips end-to-end with diagonal seams until the length is 12" longer than the distance around the quilt top. Fold and press in half lengthwise for a double binding. Sew binding to quilt.

16. Make a label to identify this quilt as being your art and attach a sleeve for hanging. Enjoy.

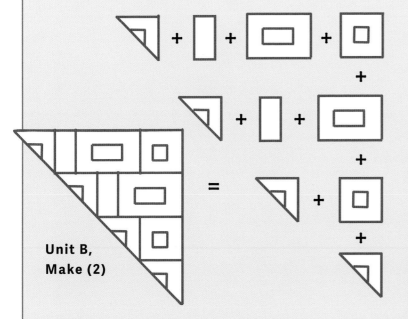

Unit B, Make (2)

INSIDE OUT, INKED!

Graphic is the one word that describes **Inside Out, Inked**! This is accomplished by placing each colorway together to increase the intensity. To keep the huge 4-patch from being predictable, the center segments change colors in each quadrant. Edgy, contemporary and graphic…now I'm at three words.

SUPPLIES

- (24) 2½" x 40" strips, colorway A
- (24) 2½" x 40" strips, colorway B
- (4) 18" x 22" assorted fabrics (C, D, E and F)
- ⅔ yard binding

COMPONENT	QUANTITY
BRICKS	32
COBBLESTONES	32
3½" PEBBLES	4

From Each Colorway

- Using (16) strips, cut (2) 2½" x 9½" and (2) 2½" x 2½" from each strip for the Bricks.
- Using (8) strips, cut (4) 2½" x 6½" and (4) 2½" x 2½" from each strip for the Cobblestones.

From Each 18" x 22" Fabric C

- Cut (1) 3½" strip, crosscut (1) 3½" x 3½" Pebble.
- Cut (3) 2½" x 22" strips, crosscut (8) 2½" x 5½" and (8) 2½" x 2½" segments.

INSTRUCTIONS

1. Make (8) Bricks using colorway A. For each Brick, select (2) 2½" x 9½" and (2) 2½" x 2½" of one fabric. Use (1) 2½" x 5½" of fabric C for the center.

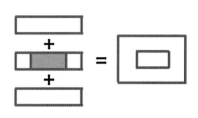

2. Make (8) Cobblestones using colorway A. For each Cobblestone, select (2) 2½" x 6½" and (2) 2½" x 2½" of the fabric. Use (1) 2½" x 2½" of fabric C for the center.

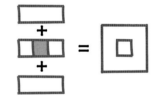

3. Stitch one Cobblestone to the end of each Brick.

4. Lay out per sketch and stitch together to complete units. Make (4) Units: A1, A2, A3, A4.

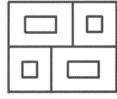

Units: A1 and A3

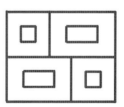

Units: A2 and A4

5. Lay out Units per sketch with the 3½" fabric C Pebble in the center.

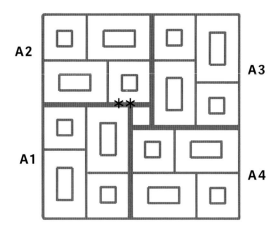

6. Start with a partial seam (**) by sewing the 3½" Pebble to Unit A1; stitch only about 2" from the top. Press seam toward Unit A1.

7. Stitch Unit A2 across Unit A1/Pebble. Press seam toward Unit A2.

8. Stitch Unit A3 across Unit A2/Pebble. Press seam toward Unit A3.

9. Stitch Unit A4 across Unit A3/Pebble. Press seam toward Unit A4.

10. Now complete the partial seam (**) between Unit A4 and Unit A2/Pebble.

11. Repeat steps 1-10 using colorway B and fabric D.

12. Repeat steps 1-10 using colorway B and fabric E.

13. Repeat steps 1-10 using colorway A and fabric F.

14. Stitch step 10 to step 11 and step 12 to step 13. Then stitch together to form a large 4-patch.

15. Layer backing, batting and quilt top. Quilt as desired. I really think machine quilting is the way to go for this highly graphic lap quilt. Select an overall edge to edge design.

16. Make binding by connecting (7) 2½" x 40" strips end-to-end using diagonal seams. Fold and press in half lengthwise. Sew binding to quilt.

17. Make a label to identify this quilt as being your art and enjoy.

LET'S FACE IT!

Facing makes the quilt appear "frameless" and is quite effective on modern quilts. It's a great option for quilts with contoured edges. Best of all, it's quick to execute, so give it a go!

1. Cut binding 2½" x 40" and sew end to end with a diagonal seam. Press in half lengthwise.

2. Measure the quilt from side to side, cut (2) pieces of binding to this length.

3. Center and pin binding to the FRONT of the quilt at the top and bottom.

4. Stitch with a ⅜" seam allowance along the top and bottom edge.

FRONT OF QUILT

5. Measure the quilt from top to bottom, and then subtract 1"; cut (2) pieces of binding to this length.

6. Center and pin binding to the FRONT of the quilt at the sides. Stitch with ⅜" seam allowance down the entire edge.

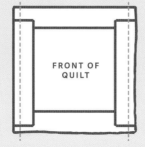

FRONT OF QUILT

7. Press all seams toward the binding. Feather binding fabric and batting to reduce the bulk in the seam allowance.

8. Trim corners…again to reduce bulk.

BACK OF QUILT

9. Turn all binding to the back of the quilt and finesse corners.

BACK OF QUILT

10. Place ½" wide double-sided lightweight fusible material between quilt back and binding.

11. Pin binding in position and press following manufacturer's instructions.

12. Appliqué binding to quilt to finish. Remove pins.

13. Press the front edge of the quilt lightly with steam. You may want to use a pressing cloth to prevent shine.

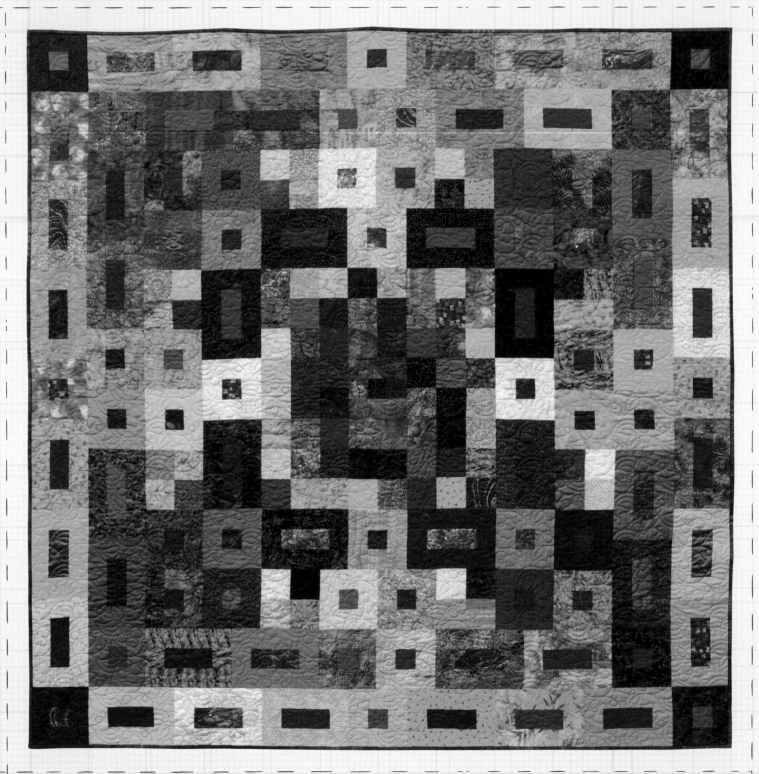

SYMMETRY SQUARE

Symmetry. When looking in a mirror, one side reflects the other. What's on left is now on the right. This is different from a repeated pattern where what is on the left is still on the left, again. However with **Symmetry Square** the challenge is to achieve a balance with an element of surprise. Maria used a variety of reds for the Pebbles to form a diagonal "X" through the center. She continued with splashes of red to harmonize the palette of the Bricks and Cobblestones. To create a stronger design line, highlight the "four mirrors" with a Soloist fabric in addition to a Harmonizer.

SUPPLIES

- (77) 2½" x 40" strips, assorted fabric
- (80) 3½" x 3½" Pebbles in assorted fabrics
- (12) 3½" x 3½" Harmonizer Pebbles
- ½ yard Harmonizer fabric or assortment of fabric. Cut 2½" strips as needed
- ⅔ yard for binding

COMPONENT	QUANTITY
BRICKS	48
COBBLESTONES	29
3½" PEBBLES	92

For Each Brick

- From (1) 2½" strip, crosscut (2) 2½" x 9½" and (2) 2½" x 2½" segments.
- From 2½" Harmonizer strip, crosscut (1) 2½" x 5½" segment.

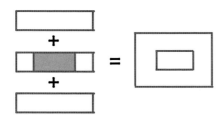

For Each Cobblestone

- From (1) 2½" strip, crosscut (2) 6½" x 2½" and (2) 2½" x 2½" segments.
- From 2½" Harmonizer strip, crosscut (1) 2½" x 2½" segment.

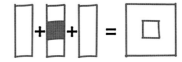

INSTRUCTIONS

Round A, Center

1. Make (1) "Reverse" Cobblestone using the Harmonizer fabric as the main body and the center square from the assortment.

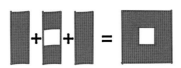

2. Using (48) 3½" assorted Pebbles, (12) 3½" Harmonizer Pebbles and reverse Cobblestone, lay out an 8 x 8 center block grid.

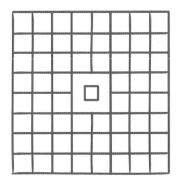

3. Stitch square to square to form rows 1, 2, 3, 6, 7 and 8.

4. For rows 4 and 5, stitch Pebbles in pairs then pairs to Cobblestone.

5. Finally stitch row to row. Matching intersections is very important so nest the seams. This forms the center of the medallion.

Round B, Border 1

6. Make (8) Bricks and (8) Cobblestones.

7. Stitch one Brick to opposite sides of (4) Cobblestones. Make (4) border units.

8. Stitch one border unit to sides of Round A. Press seam toward the border unit.

9. Stitch one Cobblestone to each end of the remaining (2) border units. Then stitch to top and bottom of Round A. Press seams toward the border units.

Round C, Border 2

10. Make (20) Cobblestones.

11. Using the remaining (32) 3½" Pebbles, stitch together into pairs. Then stitch pairs together to form a 4-Patch. Make (8) 4-patches.

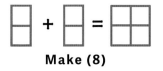

Make (8)

12. Stitch one Cobblestone to each side of the 4-Patches. Then stitch (2) together end to end. Make (4) border units.

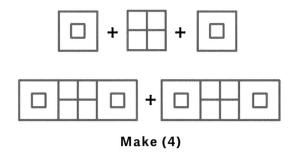

Make (4)

13. Stitch one border unit to the sides of Round B. Press seams toward the border units.

14. Stitch one Cobblestone to each end of the remaining border units. Then stitch to top and bottom of Round B. Press seam toward the border units.

Round D, Border 3

15. Make (16) Bricks and (12) Cobblestones.

16. Stitch (2) Bricks and (1) Cobblestone together. Then stitch (2) together on the Cobblestone side. Make (4) border units.

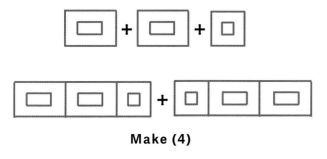

Make (4)

17. Stitch one border unit to each side of Round C. Press seams toward border units.

18. Add Cobblestones to the end of the remaining border units. Then add to the top and bottom of Round C. Press seams toward border units.

Round E, Border 4

19. Make (24) Bricks and (8) Cobblestones.

20. Stitch (3) Bricks in a row on the short sides. Then stitch to each side of a Cobblestone. Make (4) border units.

21. Stitch border units to both sides of Round D. Press seams toward border units.

22. Stitch remaining Cobblestones to each end of border units. Then stitch to top and bottom of Round D. Press seam toward border units.

23. Layer backing, batting and quilt top. Quilt as desired.

24. Make binding by connecting 2½" strips end-to-end with a diagonal seam until the length is 12" longer than the distance around the quilt top. Fold and press in half lengthwise for a double binding. Sew binding to quilt.

25. Make a label to identify this quilt as being your art. Add a hanging sleeve if you plan to hang the quilt; otherwise, enjoy!

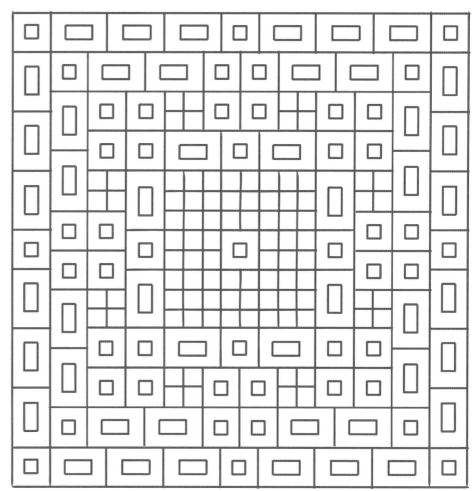

STYLIZE

Create a medallion quilt by alternating between light and dark tones round to round. Maintain strong design lines with the coloring. Use a dominant Soloist for the dark shaded squares and a blendable Harmonizer for the light shaded rectangles.

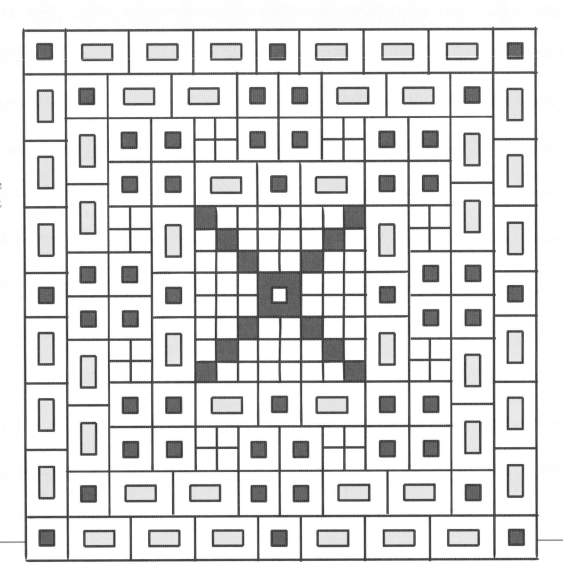

THINK SCRAPPY!

A medley of scale gets the most from pre-cuts. Blended, scraps create a new fabric. Keep the design strong. Highlight the "four mirrors" with a Soloist fabric for the center of the 9-patches.

QUILT SIZE   72" X 72"

SCRAPS	
BRICKS	48
3½" PEBBLES	80
2½" GRAVEL	392

SOLOIST	
BRICKS	
3½" PEBBLES	12
2½" GRAVEL	49

RHYME AND REASON

When I think clean up, clear out and declutter, I think scrappy. I don't need a real purpose to make a quilt and every quilt doesn't start or end in a masterpiece. Some have no rhyme or reason...yet at the end of the day, it makes me blooming happy.

SUPPLIES

- (336) 2½" x 2½" Gravel squares
- Zillions of 1½" strips
- 1 yard for border and binding
- Angle Trim Tool

From 1½" strips

- Cut (60) 1½" x 4½"
- Cut (76) 1½" x 5½"
- Cut (34) 1½" x 10½"
- Cut (34) 1½" x 12½"

From border fabric cut (8) 2" x 40" strips

- Crosscut (4) 2" x 26"
- Crosscut (4) 2" x 27½"

STRIPS	ROUND A	ROUND B
1½" X 4½"	36	24
1½" X 5½"	36	40
1½" X 10½"	18	16
1½" X 12½"	18	16
2½" X 2½" GRAVEL	144	192

INSTRUCTIONS

Round A, Center

1. Pair (144) 2½" Gravel by twos (one light and one dark) for (72) units; sew together and press seam to dark Gravel. Then stitch pairs together by twos for (36) 4-Patches. Press seam open.

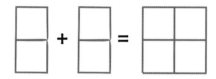

2. Stitch 1½" x 4½" strip to one side of 4-Patch. Then stitch 1½" x 5½" strip to the adjacent side. Press seams toward the strips. Make (36) units.

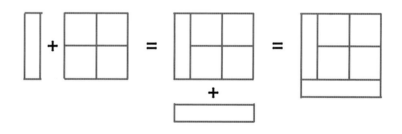

3. Stitch units together in pairs. Press seam toward the 1½" x 5½" strip.

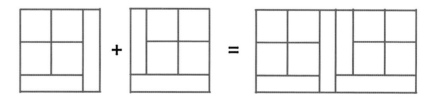

4. Then stitch pairs together, on the strip sides. Make (9) blocks.

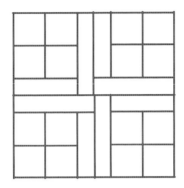

5. Stitch the 1½" x 10½" strips to opposite sides of the block. Press seams toward the strips.

6. Stitch the 1½" x 12½" strips to the top and bottom of the block. Press seams toward the strips. Make (9) bordered blocks.

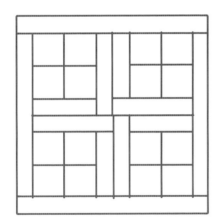

7. Assemble in a 9-patch configuration. The "A" positions have the 12½" strip on top and the "B" positions have the 10½" strip on top.

A	B	A
B	A	B
A	B	A

8. Stitch block to block to form rows. Then row to row to complete the center.

Round B, Corner

9. Make (24) units following steps 1-2.

10. Using (16) units, follow steps 3-6 to make (4) bordered blocks.

11. Select (48) 2½" Gravel squares. Make (16) Pieced Triangles, see sketch. Trim with the Angle Trim Tool. DISCARD trimmings!

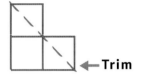

12. Stitch 1½" x 5½" strip to the LEFT side of (8) Pieced Triangles and to the RIGHT side of (8) Pieced Triangles. Press seams to the strips.

Make 8—Left   **Make 8—Right**

13. Then stitch one LEFT and one RIGHT to adjacent sides of the unit (step 9).

14. Stitch 1½" x 10½" strip to the TOP side then stitch 1½" x 12½" strip to the LEFT side. Press seams to the strips. Trim center strips with the Angle Trim Tool. DISCARD trimmings! Make (8) partial bordered blocks.

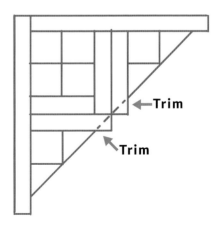

15. Stitch one partial bordered block to adjacent sides of the bordered block (step 10). Make (4) corner units.

16. Stitch 2" x 26" border strip to the LEFT side of each corner unit. Press seams toward the borders. Make (4).

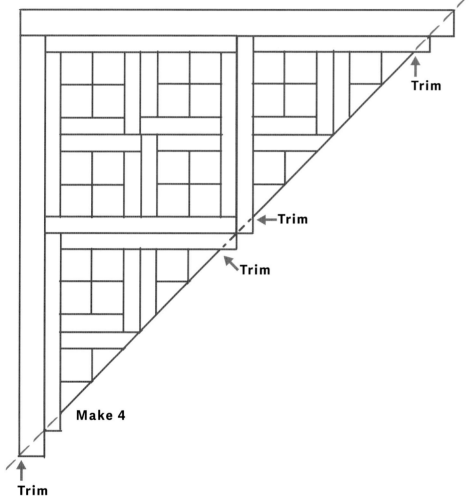

Trim

Trim

Trim

Make 4

Trim

17. Then stitch 2" x 27½" border strip to the TOP of each corner unit. Press seams toward the borders. Trim center strips and end strips with the Angle Trim Tool. Make (4) Corners.

18. Center the corners to opposite sides of Round A. Pin, Pin, Pin. Stitch and press seams toward the corners.

19. Center and pin the remaining corners to Round A. Check the alignment of outer block strips with sewn corners. The tip of Round A will float into the border. Stitch and press seams toward the corners.

20. Add free form appliqué as desired.

21. Layer backing, batting and quilt top. Then quilt as desired.

22. Make binding by connecting (6-7) 2½" strips end-to-end with diagonal seams until the length is 12" longer than the distance around the quilt top. Fold and press in half lengthwise for a double binding. Sew binding to quilt.

23. Make a label to identify this quilt as being your art. Add a hanging sleeve if you plan to hang the quilt; otherwise, enjoy!

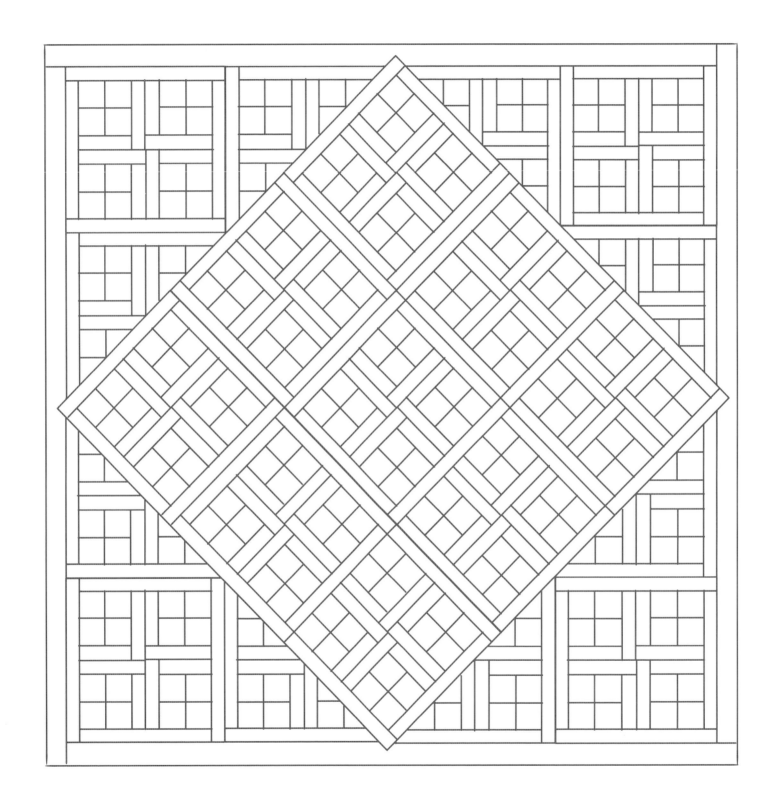

CHARM MAGIC!

A clever way to make 4-patches starting from 5" charm squares.

1. Layer (2) 5" charms, right sides together.

2. Stitch ¼" down left and right side edges.

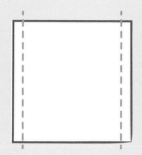

3. Cut 2½" from edge.

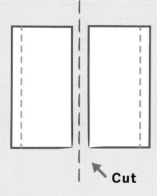

Cut

4. Press seam toward darker fabric.

5. Layer, right sides together. Make sure seams are nested and top fabric is reversed from bottom fabric.

Dark fabric on bottom   **Dark fabric on top**

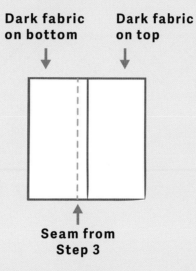

Seam from Step 3

6. Stitch ¼" across top and bottom side edges.

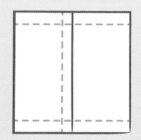

7. Cut 2½" from edge.

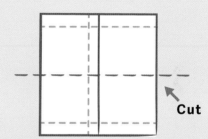

Cut

8. Press seam open. Makes (2) 4-patches.

MADE BY JO BIAGIOLI, RITA COLLEN, GAIL SCHULTZ, CHRIS WHITSELL

MAIN STREET COMMONS

It seems like every town has a main street. And in the center of these main streets there has been some amazing brick work or pavers. I combined that inspiration with a contemporary medallion layout. You decide what perspective or how many "rounds" to make. Challenge your skill by taking the quilt from square to point back to square. It will change your perspective on what's possible.

SUPPLIES

- (8) 6½" x 22" strips of assorted Bright fabrics
- (6) 18" x 22" strips of assorted Dark fabrics
- 1 yard Harmonizer fabric for 3½" Pebbles and binding
- Angle Trim Tool

COMPONENTS	QUANTITY	
6½" X 9½" RECTANGLES	8 (BRIGHT)	
6½" X 6½" SQUARES	4 (DARK)	20 (BRIGHT)
6½" TRIANGLES	32 (BRIGHT)	
3½" X 3½" SQUARES	56 (DARK)	48 (HARMONIZER)

- Crosscut the components according to the chart above. **NOTE:** From Dark fabric, cut (4) 6½" x 6½" squares first. Cut 3½" strips from the remaining fabric, then crosscut into 3½" x 3½" squares.

INSTRUCTIONS

Round A, Center

1. Using (4) 6½" x 6½" Dark squares, stitch two together for (2) pairs. Stitch pairs together to make 4-Patch.

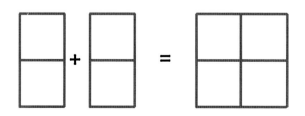

Round B, Border 1

2. Using (8) 6½" x 9½" Bright rectangles, stitch two together on the short side for (4) pairs. Using a partial seam (**), stitch rectangle pair 3½" on one side of 4-Patch.

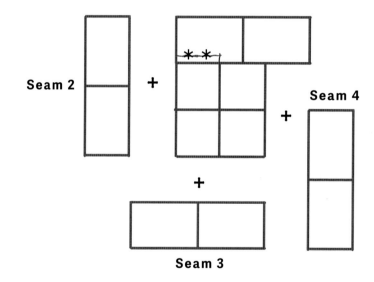

3. Then stitch a rectangle pair to the left side of unit. Continue stitching rectangle pairs counterclockwise to each side of 4-Patch.

4. Last, complete the partial seam.

Round C, Corner

5. Using (8) 3½" x 3½" Dark squares make (2) 4-Patches.

6. Using (4) 3½" x 3½" Dark squares and (8) 3½" x 3½" Harmonizer squares make (4) Pieced Triangles. Begin by stitching a Dark square to a Harmonizer square. Then stitch a Harmonizer square to unit. Trim using Angle Trim Tool.

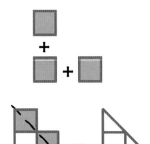

7. Stitch (2) Pieced Triangles to a 4-Patch. Make (2) units.

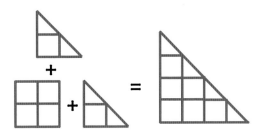

8. Stitch the (2) units together on the short side to form (1) corner.

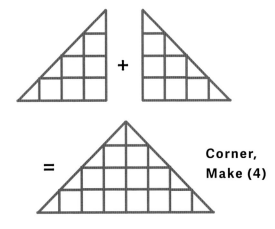

Corner, Make (4)

9. Repeat steps 5-8 to make (4) corners. Then stitch (1) corner to each side of Round B.

Round D, Border 2

10. Using (3) 6½" x 6½" Bright squares and (6) 6½" Bright Triangles stitch the center, left and right units.

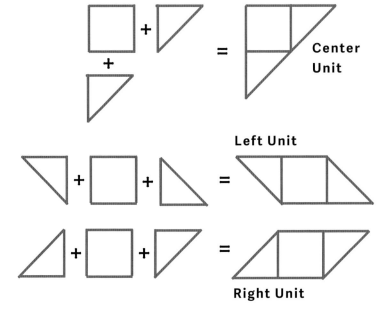

Center Unit

Left Unit

Right Unit

11. Stitch the left unit to the center unit then stitch the right unit to the center unit. Make (4). Then stitch to each side of Round C.

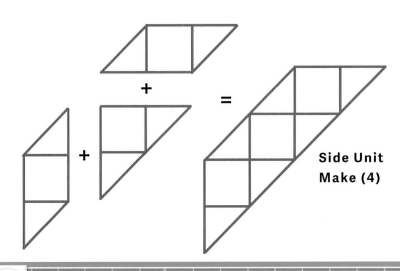

Side Unit Make (4)

12. Using (2) 3½" x 3½" Dark squares and (4) 3½" x 3½" Harmonizer squares make (2) Pieced Triangles. Stitch the Pieced Triangles together on the short side.

13. Using (2) 6½" x 6½" Bright squares and (2) 6½" Bright Triangles stitch the following:

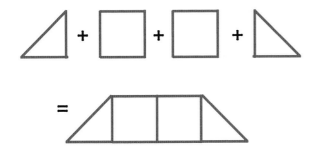

14. Stitch the Pieced Triangle unit to the Bright unit.

15. Repeat steps 12-14 to make (4) corner units. Stitch to complete the corners of Round D. Quilt will measure approximately 50" x 50".

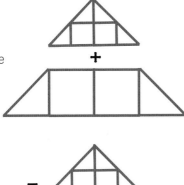

CAUTION: The entire outside edges of the quilt are on bias. To control stretching stay-stitch ¼" from the edge to maintain shape or add 2" final border using the Harmonizer fabric before layering or quilting.

16. Layer backing, batting and quilt top. Quilt as desired.

17. Make binding by connecting 2½" strips end-to-end with diagonal seams until the length is 12" longer than the distance around the quilt top. Fold and press in half lengthwise for a double binding. Sew binding to quilt.

18. Make a label to identify this quilt as being your art; add a hanging sleeve. Enjoy.

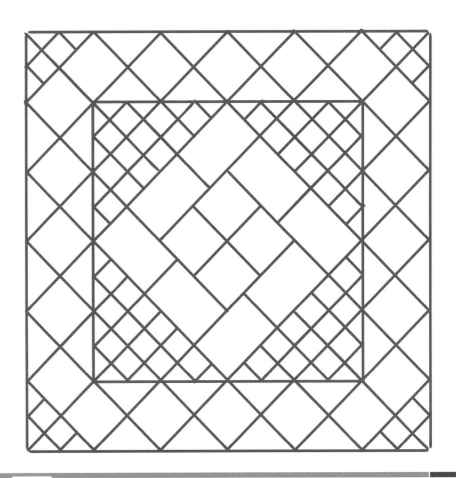

GO BACK TO SQUARE

For a 72" x 72" let's go back to square by adding Round E, Corners. Full instructions are on page 122.

The beauty of having a medallion design is you can choose your perspective by adding or omitting rounds. Adding corners to the Modern version not only increases the size, it also changes the perspective. Just follow the layout sketch and quantity table for the bonus Round E, Corners. Use the stitching schematic for step 16, page 122.

6½" x 9½" BRIGHT RECTANGLES	16
6½" x 6½" BRIGHT SQUARES	12
6½" x 6½" DARK SQUARES	16
6½" BRIGHT TRIANGLES	8
3½" x 3½" DARK SQUARES	48
3½" x 3½" HARMONIZER SQUARES	32

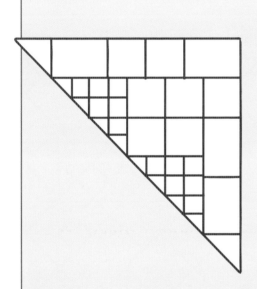

Modern Round E, Corner

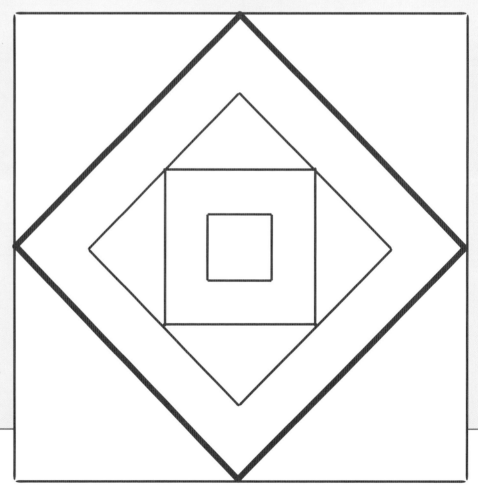

CONTEMPORARY

A CHANGE OF PERSPECTIVE... *Back to square by adding Round E*

MADE BY

CORNELIA J. NYHOF

QUILTED BY

BONNIE RHOBY

SUPPLIES

- (10) 18" x 22" assorted Choir fabrics
- 2 yards Harmonizer fabric
- ⅔ yard binding fabric
- Angle Trim Tool

BRICKS	24
COBBLESTONES	48
HALF-COBBLESTONES	24
6½" TRIANGLES	24
3½" x 3½" CHOIR SQUARES	112
3½" x 3½" HARMONIZER SQUARES	64

Follow "Construction Master Class" for component construction. Page 17.

For Each Brick

- From (1) 2½" Choir strip, crosscut (2) 2½" x 9½" and (2) 2½" x 2½" segments.
- From a 2½" Harmonizer strip, crosscut (1) 2½" x 5½" segment.
- Make (24) Bricks.

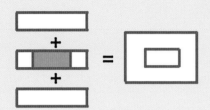

For Each Cobblestone

- From (1) 2½" Choir strip, crosscut (2) 2½" x 6½" and (2) 2½" x 2½" segments.
- From a 2½" Harmonizer strip, crosscut (1) 2½" x 2½" segment.
- Make (48) Cobblestones.

For Two Half-Cobblestones

- From (1) 2½" Choir strip, crosscut (1) 2½" x 6½" and (2) 2½" x 2½" segments.
- From a 2½" Harmonizer strip, crosscut (1) 2½" x 2½" segment.
- Make (1) Brick.
- Using the Angle Trim Tool, trim twice to make (2) Half-Cobblestones.
- Make (24) Half-Cobblestones.

INSTRUCTIONS

Round A, Center

1. Using (16) 3½" x 3½" Choir squares, make (4) 4-Patches. Stitch (2) 4-Patches together to form a 16-Patch Round A Center.

Round B, Border 1

2. Using (8) Bricks, stitch two together on the short side for (4) pairs. Using a partial seam (**), stitch one Brick pair 3" on one side of Round A.

3. Then stitch a Brick pair to the left side of Round A. Continue stitching Brick pairs counterclockwise to each side of Round A.

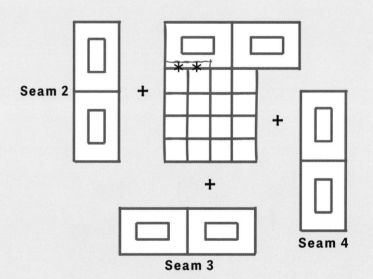

4. Lastly, complete the partial seam.

Round C, Corners

5. Using (8) 3½" x 3½" Choir squares make (2) 4-patches.

6. Using (4) 3½" x 3½" Choir squares and (8) 3½" x 3½" Harmonizer squares make (4) Pieced Triangles. Begin by stitching a dark square to Harmonizer square then a Harmonizer square to assembly. Trim using Angle Trim Tool. Make (4) Pieced Triangles.

7. Stitch (2) Pieced Triangles to the 4-Patch. Make (2).

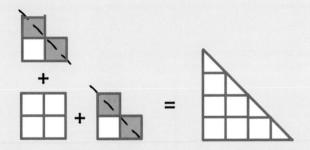

8. Stitch the (2) assemblies together on the short side to form (1) corner.

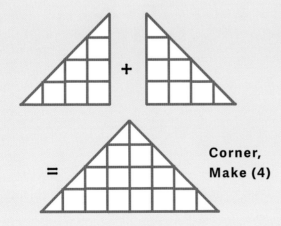

Corner, Make (4)

9. Repeat steps 5-8 to make (4) corners. Then stitch (1) corner to each side of Round B.

Round D, Border 2

10. Using (3) Cobblestones, (2) Half-Cobblestones and (2) 6½" Triangles stitch following sketch:

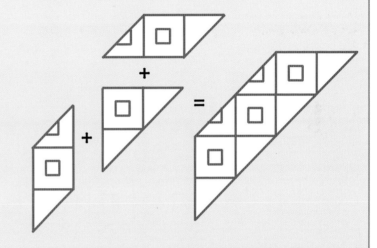

11. Make (4) then stitch to each side of Round C.

12. Using (2) Cobblestones and (4) Half-Cobblestones stitch together to form a large Pieced Triangle corner.

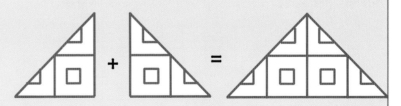

13. Repeat steps 10-12 to make (4) corners. Then stitch to complete the corners of Round D.

Round E, Corners

14. Using (8) 3½" x 3½" Choir squares make (2) 4-Patches.

15. Using (4) 3½" x 3½" Choir squares and (8) 3½" x 3½" Harmonizer squares make (4) Pieced Triangles following step 6.

16. Using (4) Bricks, (7) Cobblestones, (2) 6½" Harmonizer Triangles, (2) 4-Patches, and (4) Pieced Triangles stitch following the sketch to assemble the corner.

17. Repeat steps 14-16 to make (4) corners; then center the corner to each side of Round D and stitch.

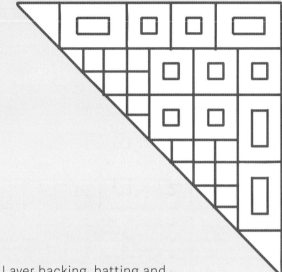

18. Layer backing, batting and quilt top. Quilt as desired.

19. Make binding by connecting 2½" strips end-to-end with diagonal seams until the length is 12" longer than the distance around the quilt top. Fold and press in half lengthwise for a double binding. Sew binding to quilt.

20. Make a label to identify this quilt as being your art. Enjoy.

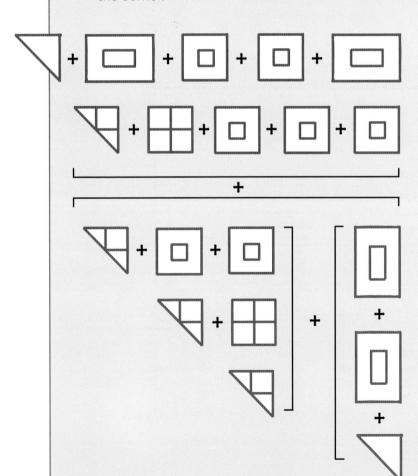

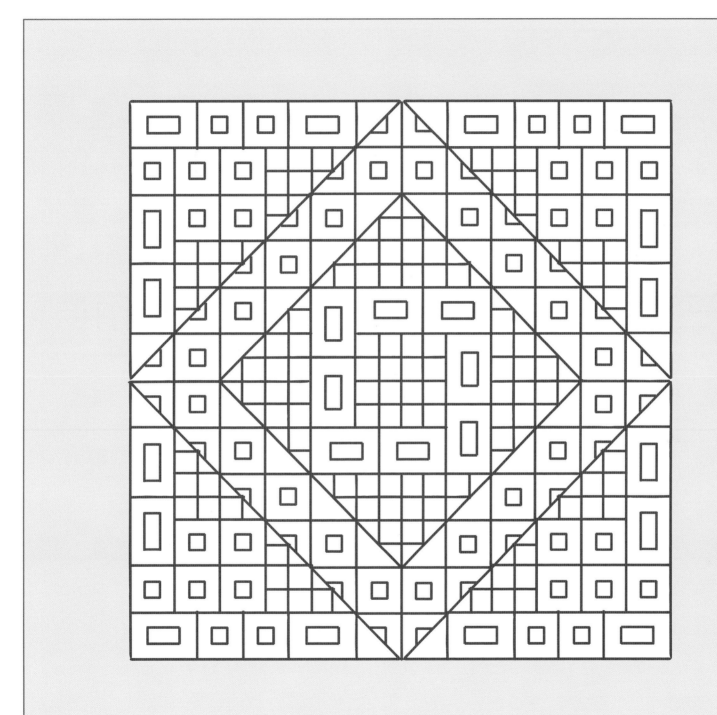

ODDS, ENDS, AND LEFTOVERS

As the title implies, challenge yourself to use up all the pre-cut squares and strips you have stored. This is a very scrappy project so go big and bold and just sew. Now if letting go and going wild scares you, certainly you can "stylize" your color scheme. Get it done and have fun!

SUPPLIES

- Zillions of 2½" squares
- Some 3½" and 4" squares
- Some 2½" and 1½" strips
- Angle Trim Tool

How many you need of what component is provided in the table below. Don't let the numbers scare you. Take it one step at a time so you're not overwhelmed. The first size is the base and for each size larger you need more stuff. Stay on course to use up all that you have stored.

You don't need to make a decision now. Plan to make the 57" x 57", then decide if you will keep going to get to the next size, or go all the way to the largest size.

QUILT SIZE	57" X 57"	57" X 75"	75" X 75"
2½" X 18" STRIPS	24		
1½" X 40" STRIPS	2		
3½" sq PEBBLES	96	+66	+86
4" sq PEBBLES+	60		
2½" sq GRAVEL	304	+72	+96

For Each Cobblestone

- Using (1) 2½" strip, cut (2) 2½" x 6½" and (2) 2½" x 2½".
- Select (1) 2½" square for the center.

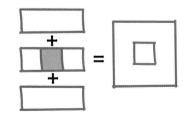

INSTRUCTIONS

Round A, Center

1. Using (64) 2½" squares, lay out an 8 x 8 block grid and stitch square to square then row to row. Matching intersections is very important so nest the seams. This forms the center of the medallion.

2. Using the (2) 1½" x 40" strips, border the center. Measure center from top to bottom. Crosscut (2) strips to this length and stitch to the sides of the center. Press seams toward the border.

3. Measure center from side to side. Crosscut (2) strips to this length and stitch to the top and bottom of the center. Press seams toward the border.

4. Square up (trim) to 17½" square.

Round B, Corner

5. Make (24) Cobblestones using the 2½" x 18" strips and 2½" squares. *I used the same color for my centers but you can choose differently.*

6. Select (24) 3½" squares. Make (8) Pieced Triangles, see sketch. Trim with the Angle Trim Tool. DISCARD trimmings!

7. Stitch (2) Pieced Triangles to Cobblestones. Press seams toward the Pieced Triangles. Make (4) units.

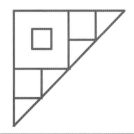

8. Stitch one unit to each side of Round A. Pin beginning, middle and end to prevent stretching.

Round C, Corner

9. Select (60) 4" squares; divide into (4) groups. Stitch together square to square and row to row to form a Pieced Triangle with 5, 4, 3, 2, 1 squares in each row; see sketch. Make (4) Pieced Triangles.

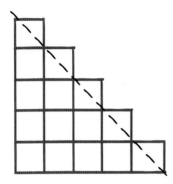

10. Trim the long side using the Angle Trim Tool for a straight edge. Place the tool on the FRONT of the Pieced Triangle. Starting at the bottom lay the tool such that the tool markings align with the pieced seams. Trim. Continue to trim from square to square. If you attempt to do the whole long edge with a big ruler the results are not as accurate. DISCARD trimmings!

11. Lay center medallion on a flat surface and GENTLY center (1) Pieced Triangle along the edge. Pin in position. Stitch. Press seam toward the Pieced Triangle. Repeat to complete each of the remaining (3) corners.

12. Measure the medallion and trim to 34½" unfinished. Hint: Measure (17¼") from the center to the edge on all (4) sides; trim excess.

Round D, Border 1

13. Divide (240) 2½" squares into groups of (6). Make (40) Pieced Triangles by stitching square to square then row to row with 3, 2, 1 squares in each row. Trim with Angle Trim Tool. Discard trimmings!

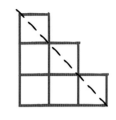

14. Stitch (6) Pieced Triangles to (3) Cobblestones; then stitch together to form border segment, see sketch. Make (4).

15. Center and stitch border segment to sides of Round C. Press seams toward border.

16. Lay out (2) Cobblestones and (4) Pieced Triangles, see sketch. Stitch (2) Cobblestones together.

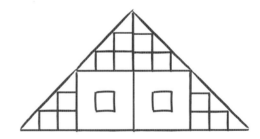

17. Stitch top (2) Pieced Triangles together on the short side.

18. Stitch the Cobblestone assembly to the triangle assembly.

19. Add a Pieced Triangle to each side of assembly. You now have a huge Pieced Triangle.

20. Repeat steps 16-19 to make (4) border corners.

21. Stitch to corners of Round D. Quilt should measure approximately 51½".

FOR 57" X 57" QUILT

Round E, Border 2

22. Using (72) 3½" squares. Sew (17) squares end to end. Make (2). Stitch to top and bottom of Round D. Press seam toward this border.

23. Using remaining squares, sew (19) squares end to end. Make (2). Stitch to each side of Round D. Press seam toward this border.

FOR 57" X 75" QUILT

Round F, Border 3

24. Make (12) 9-Patch blocks using 2½" squares.

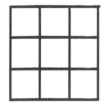

25. Using (28) 3½" squares, sew together in pairs; make (14) pairs.

26. Stitch (7) pairs between (6) 9-Patch blocks beginning and ending with the pairs. Make (2).

27. Stitch to top and bottom of Round E. Press seam towards Round E.

28. Using (38) 3½" squares, sew (19) squares end to end. Make (2). Stitch to top and bottom of quilt. Press seam toward this border.

FOR 75" X 75" QUILT

29. Make (16) 9-Patch blocks using 2½" squares.

30. Using (36) 3½" squares, sew together in pairs; make (18) pairs.

31. Stitch (9) pairs between (8) 9-Patch blocks beginning and ending with the pairs. Make (2).

32. Stitch to each side of quilt. Press seam towards Round E.

33. Using (50) 3½" squares. Sew (25) squares end to end. Make (2). Stitch to each side of quilt. Press seam toward this border.

34. Layer backing, batting and quilt top. Quilt as desired.

35. Make binding by connecting 2½" strips end-to-end with diagonal seams until the length is 12" longer than the distance around the quilt top. Fold and press in half lengthwise for a double binding. Sew binding to quilt.

36. Make a label to identify this quilt as being your art. Add a hanging sleeve if you plan to hang the quilt; otherwise, enjoy.

THINK MODERN!

SIMPLIFY. Decrease the amount of piecing and increase the impact of each element.

VARY. Add variation within the Pebbles and Gravel squares to entertain the eye.

GO GRAPHIC. Use solids and color to structure each round.

QUILT SIZE	75" X 75"
1½" X 40" STRIPS	2
6½" squares	52
6½" triangles	48
4" squares	60
3½" squares	224
2½" squares	64

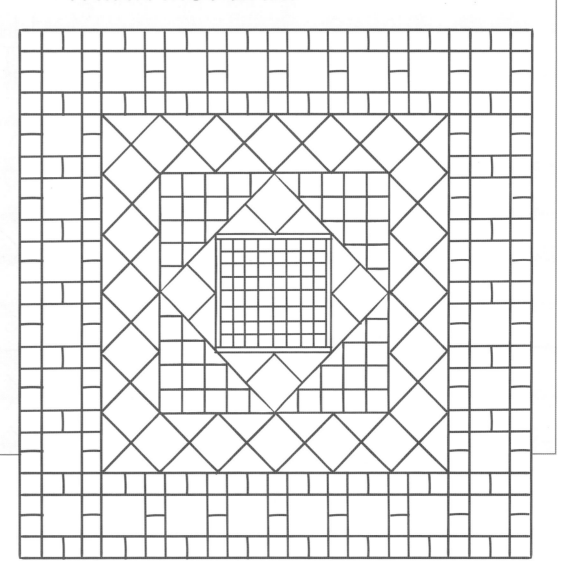

PICK UP STICKS

I looked around my studio...mostly at the mess and disorder. It was time to pick up, put away, or throw away. I had BAGS (Yes, plural! Yes, capital!) of leftovers from all the quilt tops and backs that went into Bricks, Cobblestones and Pebbles. I was torn between what to do and how to start when the idea came to design one more; the last quilt for the book that would use it up! Sticks, those little slivers of fabric, became my mortar. It was a blast to stitch and, for one shining moment, my studio was clean.

SUPPLIES

- One pound of 2½" x 20" strips
- Quarter pound of 1½" x 15" strips
- (50 or so) 2½" x 2½" Gravel
- (160) 3½" x 3½" Pebbles
- ⅔ yard binding fabric

COMPONENTS	ROUND A	ROUND B	ROUND C	ROUND D	ROUND E
(3) 2½" X 6½" SQUARES		8	16	32	40
6½" PINWHEELS (CORNERS)	4	4	4	4	4
(1) 2½" X 6½" (UNIT 1)		8			8
(2) 2½" X 6½" (UNIT 2)			8		

For 2½" Strata using 1½" strips

- Stitch (2) 1½" strips together lengthwise being careful not to stretch either of them. Press seam to one side. Trim ends even. Add a 2½" Gravel to connect strata segments. Continue creating 2½" strata as needed throughout the project to use as Mortar.

For 6½" Strata using 2½" strips

- Select (3) 2½" strips approximately the same length. Stitch (2) 2½" strips together lengthwise being careful not to stretch either of them. Press seam to one side. Stitch (1) 2½" strip to the pair beginning at the same end. Press seam to one side. Crosscut every 6½" to make 6½" x 6½" squares. Continue creating 6½" strata as needed throughout the project.

INSTRUCTIONS

Round A, Center

1. Select (2) 3½" pebbles. Mark a diagonal line on the wrong side of the lighter fabric. Put right sides together, stitch on the diagonal line. Trim ¼" on ONE side of the diagonal line and press towards the darker triangle to make (1) Half-Square Triangle.

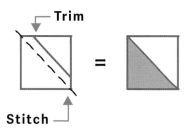

2. Repeat step 1 to make (4) Half-Square Triangles.

3. Lay out (4) Half-Square Triangles as follows then stitch (2) together to form pairs. Then stitch pairs together to form a Pinwheel.

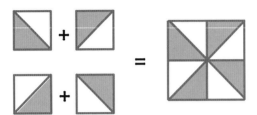

4. Square the Pinwheel to 6½" x 6½" unfinished.

5. Stitch (4) Pinwheels together in pairs then stitch pair to pair to form a 4-Patch center.

6. For Mortar, create 2½" strata using 1½" strips. Cross-cut (2) 2½" x 12½" Mortar strips and stitch to the sides of the center. Press seams toward Mortar.

7. Crosscut (2) 2½" x 16½" Mortar strips and stitch to top and bottom of center. Press seams toward Mortar.

Round B, Border (32" square)

8. Repeat steps 1-4 to make (4) Pinwheels.

9. Make (8) 6½" strata squares.

10. Select several 2½" strips, crosscut (8) 2½" x 6½" Unit 1s.

11. Lay out round B per the full sketch.

NOTE: Begin and end each side with Unit 1.

12. Stitch components to make the side borders. Stitch to the left and right of round A. Press seams.

13. Stitch components for make the top and bottom borders. The corner Pinwheels are part of the top and bottom border assemblies. Stitch border to the top and bottom of round A. Press seams.

14. For Mortar, crosscut (2) 2½" x 28½" Mortar strips and stitch to the sides of the round. Press seams toward Mortar.

15. Crosscut (2) 2½" x 32½" Mortar strips and stitch to top and bottom of the round. Press seams toward Mortar.

Round C, Border (48" square)

16. Repeat steps 1-4 to make (4) Pinwheels.

17. Make (16) 6½" strata squares.

18. Select (2) 2½" strips, stitch together lengthwise. Press seam to one side. Crosscut (8) 4½" x 6½" Unit 2s.

19. Lay out round C per the full sketch.

> **NOTE:** Begin and end each side with Unit 2.

20. Stitch components to make the side borders. Stitch to the left and right of round B. Press seams.

21. Stitch components to make the top and bottom borders. The corner Pinwheels are part of the top and bottom border assemblies. Stitch to the top and bottom of round B. Press seams.

22. For Mortar, crosscut (2) 2½" x 44½" Mortar strips and stitch to the sides of the round. Press seams toward Mortar.

23. Crosscut (2) 2½" x 48½" Mortar strips and stitch to top and bottom of the round. Press seams toward Mortar.

Round D, Border (64" square)

24. Repeat steps 1-4 to make (4) Pinwheels.

25. Make (32) 6½" strata squares.

26. Lay out round D per the full sketch.

27. Stitch components to make the side borders. Stitch to the left and right of round C. Press seams.

28. Stitch components for make the top and bottom borders. The corner Pinwheels are a part of the top and bottom border assemblies. Stitch to the top and bottom of round C. Press seams.

29. For Mortar, crosscut (2) 2½" x 60½" Mortar strips and stitch to the sides of the round. Press seams toward Mortar.

30. Crosscut (2) 2½" x 64½" Mortar strips and stitch to top and bottom of the round. Press seams toward Mortar.

Round E, Border (80" square)

31. Repeat steps 1-4 to make (4) Pinwheels.

32. Make (40) 6½" strata squares.

33. Select several 2½" strips, crosscut (8) 2½" x 6½" Unit 1s.

34. Lay out round E per the full sketch.

> **NOTE:** Begin and end each side with Unit 1.

35. Stitch components to make the side borders. Stitch to the left and right of round D. Press seams.

36. Stitch components to make the top and bottom borders. The corner Pinwheels are part of the top and bottom border assemblies. Stitch to the top and bottom of round D. Press seams.

37. For Mortar, crosscut (2) 2½" x 76½" Mortar strips and stitch to the sides of the round. Press seams toward Mortar.

38. Crosscut (2) 2½" x 80½" Mortar strips and stitch to top and bottom of the round. Press seams toward Mortar.

39. Layer backing, batting and quilt top. Quilt as desired.

40. Make binding by connecting 2½" strips end-to-end with diagonal seams until the length is 12" longer than the distance around the quilt top. Fold and press in half lengthwise for a double binding. Sew binding to quilt.

41. Make a label to identify this quilt as being your art and enjoy!

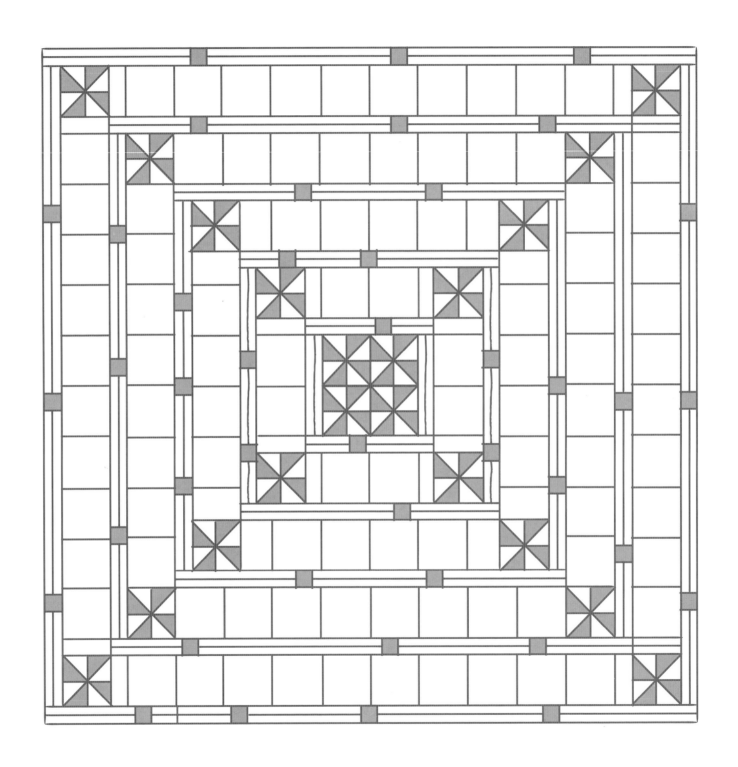

TIME IS ON YOUR SIDE...YES IT IS

Making a scrap quilt depends on the quantity and size of your scraps, and the available time. For me having alternative components is the name of the game. As I see it, choosing another path is okay by me.

	QUICK	REASONABLE*	GOT TIME ON MY HANDS
SQUARES	6½" X 6½"	(3) 2½" X 6½"	(6) 1½" X 6½"
CORNERS	(4) 3½" X 3½"	6½" PINWHEEL	6½" SPIDERWEB
MORTAR	(1) 2½" STRIPS	(2) 1½" STRIPS	(2) 1½" STRIPS
UNIT A	(1) 2½" X 6½"	(1) 2½" X 6½"	(2) 1½" X 6½"
UNIT B	(1) 2½" X 6½"	(2) 2½" X 6½"	(4) 1½" X 6½"

***Pick Up Sticks** uses the entire "Reasonable" option.

THE SPECIALISTS

ASHLEY MALINOWSKI

Ashley Malinowski started sewing when her mother took her to multiple summer camps from the age of 6. By 12, Ashley got bit by the longarming bug because she was tired of always stitching in the ditch for her Delaware State Fair quilts. That is when she discovered a longarm quilting machine rental program.

After using the machine several times, she headed to the Machine Quilting Expo (MQX) in Rhode Island her senior year of high school. She came home with a longarm to start her own business in June of 2010. Ever since, Ashley continues to longarm, both edge-to-edge designs and custom for customers and loves every minute of it.

Ashley can be reached through her website, midnightquilter.weebly.com and has a strong Facebook presence at Midnight Quilter.

JUDY M. CLARK

Judy M. Clark started sewing as a very young girl when her sister-in-law taught her how to make dresses. After her two children were raised and on their own, Judy decided to try quilt making and her husband bought her an embroidery machine. She was instantly addicted! In 2010, he bought her a longarm after seeing what a local quilter did. He told her, "You need to do this!" and she has been quilting for herself and customers ever since.

A retired Certified Dental Assistant, Judy enjoys being available to help with her 5 grandsons. She loves the creative aspect of quilting and is always amazed how they turn out. Judy can be reached at jclark_1970@ msn.com or through her website, hillside-quiltingonline.com. Join her on Facebook at Hillside Quilting, LLC.

MELANIE BARRETT

Melanie Barrett has been quilting since 2000. She began sewing as a young girl and was first exposed to quiltmaking through friends in high school. Life continued from college to marriage with two children and a move to Houston, Texas before she stepped into her first quilt shop. Intrigued, she decided now was the time and signed up for a Bargello class. The quilting bug had taken hold.

Melanie worked at several quilt shops before she decided to open the doors of Quilt Essentials. Today, she is moving her shop in a different direction with strictly an online business. Melanie says, "Quilting has brought a lot of awesome things into my life, but the best has been the friendships." She is not sure where this new path will lead, however she is enjoying the journey.

Visit Melanie at her website www.quiltessentialsonline.com or contact her at quiltessentials@live.com.

MARIA O'HAVER

Maria O'Haver has always been interested in various crafts, but since her first visit to a quilt shop about 20 years ago, quilt making has become a favorite activity. She took various quilting classes over the years to learn about the huge variety of techniques and improve her skills.

In 2005, her love of quilting developed into a full time business with the purchase of a Gammill long arm machine.

Her business, Pangor Quilt Design Studio, has grown to two machines and is now taking most of the first floor of her house. She thoroughly enjoys quilting for customers, but still finds time to use her creative energy to make her own quilts.

Maria's website is www.mariaohaver.com.

CHARLOTTE NOLL

Charlotte Noll is a quilt artist that loves fabric, thread, buttons, and beads. Charlotte has been quilting since 1980 and has made many traditional and art quilts, however today, her eye is on tracking the modern quilting style.

A fierce competitor, she can't pass up a challenge or call for entry. Her quilt featured in *Bricks, Cobblestones and Pebbles*, Debby's Modern X, has been juried into several 2016 American Quilting Society (AQS) shows including the prestigious, Paducah. Debby's Modern X received 2nd Place award honors in the Wall-Modern category at the 2016 AQS Phoenix show.

Visit Charlotte and see her artistry on Instagram at instagram.com/kirkenoll/.

CORNELIA NYHOF

Cornelia (Elly) Nyhof has been sewing for as long as she can remember and has been quilting since 1989.

Elly "met" Gyleen online by being the first person from Michigan to order The Dream from Gyleen's website. Since this serendipitous beginning Elly has participated in several of Gyleen's online poetry and quilt challenges with outstanding results. She is a contributor to "In This House" haiku poetry book and her Trash to Treasure Pineapple challenge quilt was juried into the 2010 special exhibit of the International Quilt Festival—Long Beach and Houston. In addition, Gyleen's pattern , Canal Street Tiles, earned her Blue ribbon at the 2014 American Quilters Society show and was featured in their 2015 AQS Engagement Calendar.

Elly says, "I love all aspects of quilting, including the dreaded, appliqué! However, through quilting and the West Michigan Quilt Guild, I have met and made the most amazing friends! Quilters are some of the most loving and giving people I am privileged to know."

JUDY WILSON

From her oldest memory, Judy Wilson had an interest in sewing and other textile arts. A true "Needlewoman," her passion extends through needlepoint, quilting and garment making. Judy says she never met a fiber she didn't like. She holds a Bachelor of Science degree in Clothing and Textiles from Virginia Tech. Oddly enough, there was only one sewing class offered, Tailoring. She recently completed a French-style couture jacket, a project that had a life of its own. It gave her a true appreciation of the creations from the top fashion houses in Europe.

Judy recalls that her first quilt didn't hold up. The unbleached muslin patches in her quilt simply wore out. No longer a novice, she now knows what it means to use good fabric. The lesson from that experience has remained with Judy throughout her needle art journey.

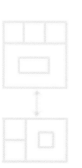
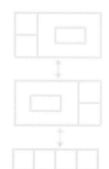

ACKNOWLEDGMENTS

It has been a blessing to design, teach and lecture about quilts and quiltmaking. However, it has been a greater blessing to be in the presence of quilters across the country like Julie Renken that cheer me on, inspire me and embrace my designs. Without those thousands of quilters my climb up this pile of quilts wouldn't be as sweet. Thank you all from the depths of my soul.

When the chips are down and you're out of time is when you call on "The Specialist." Thank you, Melanie Barrett, Judy Clark, Charlotte Noll, Cornelia Nyhof and Maria O'Haver for saving my sanity by making quilts without hesitation. Then there was the early morning rendezvous in a parking lot with Ashley Malinowski who provided the 24-hour pick up to drop off of the machine quilting; thank you Ashley for your commitment to "get it done."

In the middle of producing *Bricks, Cobblestones and Pebbles*, there were new fun challenges. Thank you, Karey Bresenhan, Founder, President and CEO, and Judy Murrah, Vice President of Administration and Education, of QUILTS, Inc., parent company of the International Quilt Festival, Inc. (IQF) for selecting me to be one of the team leaders for the Iron Quilter Competition. And to the Take Five team: Rita Collen, Tammy Westfall, Becky Wigg and Jessica Wigg who expertly put the hammer down when they provided the "Modern" edge to **So Square** during the Chicago show. Oh, what fun and a super sweet WIN! As if that wasn't blessing enough, thank you Karey Bresenhan for sponsoring and the Special Exhibit Coordinators, Becky Navarro and Deann Shamuyarira, for navigating me though my first curated special exhibit, **Odds, Ends and Leftovers**. Again and again, IQF has put me firmly on the global quilting map and I am humbly grateful.

When I asked for industry support BERNINA, Pellon, Aurifil and Red Rooster Fabrics said yes. Jeannine Cook-Delpit from BERNINA America, upgraded my B440 to the sleek high tech B580… dream machine. Erin Sampson, Pellon USA, made sure the 100% cotton Legacy batting was in supply; it's the guts that bring each quilt to life. I can't say enough about Alex Veronelli from Aurifil who not only generously provided 50wt thread for my piecing, but also to each student in my IQF-Houston workshops. I didn't think I could be a thread snob but Aurifil keeps my stitches smooth and seams flat. Last but far from least is Anna Fishkin of Red Rooster Fabrics. When Anna showed me the Inked Fabric collection I said, "WOW!" And Anna said, "I'll send you some." This collection inspired the design **Inside Out, Inked!** Thank you all for your sponsorship and for being instrumental in the production of the quilts for *Bricks, Cobblestones and Pebbles*.

The *Bricks, Cobblestone and Pebbles* production team is one of the best! Brian Boehm (and Kellie) of iDesign Graphics have traveled this path with me more than once. Brian's creative talent, patience and insight can't be matched. He has taken my vision from concept to reality. Thank you, thank you…you're the best! The trio of editors, Gail Evans Tilton, Gail F. Johnson and Holly Kravec have made my thoughts complete. They fixed my syntax errors and generally made the book sound and flow with ease. Thank you; your talent and experience are invaluable.

I run through every emotion humanly possible when producing a book. It's my parents and close friends that magically appear to keep me grounded with confidence. Thanks to Peg Bingham, Joyce Baker Brown, Janice Edmonds Scott, Alice Kish and Judy Wilson for lending me your ear and for providing priceless business advice. And thanks to the one and only Holly Kravec who kept the business running when my brain was on overload. You always found the files, had the number when it mattered most.

And finally to my biggest fan, the love of my life and closest ally, Raymond C.H. McGowan, who loved me through it all… and takes a fabulous photograph I might add. Huge hug, big smile…yes, it's done. My deepest gratitude and thanks.

IN COLOURFUL STITCHES…GYLEEN

DEBBIE ADAMI, SHANNON MCGRAW, AUIAN WARD, AND MARY JO YACKLEY

IRON QUILTER TEAM: RITA COLLEN, TAMMY WESTFALL, BECKY WIGG, AND JESSICA WIGG

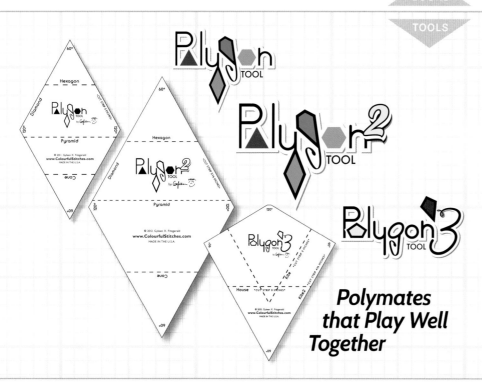
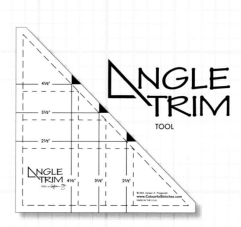

GYLEEN X. FITZGERALD

GYLEEN FITZGERALD makes quilts that blend color, pattern and texture to provide a contemporary essence in traditional quilting. Her strength as a quilter is demonstrated by the infusion of engineering tools and innovative techniques to simplify visually complex quilts. She shares her enthusiasm for quilting through interactive lectures and workshops. As a writer, Gyleen centers on quilt project books and how-to videos, magazine articles, haiku poetry, and children's books.

An avid quilter, Gyleen has earned Best of Show honors and as a publisher, she is a Gold Medal winner for *Polygon Affair…So Easy You'll Fall in Love* and *Quilts: Unfinished Stories with New Endings*.

She is best known for inspiring *Trash to Treasure Pineapple Quilts* and the creation of the **Pineapple Tool** by Gyleen.

Gyleen has appeared on The Quilt Show and Lifetime TV promoting a contemporary spirit in traditional quiltmaking.

For Gyleen, dreams hold no limits. Ray, her husband is her shining light and quilting is her passion; together her life is in balance.

Gyleen is a Philadelphia, PA native who spent her formative years in Taiwan and Japan.

SIGNATURE COLOR IS RED

 LOVES THE WARMTH AND DRAPE OF LEGACY 100% COTTON BATTING

SEWING MACHINE OF CHOICE IS BERNINA 580

 BIG STITCHES WITH PRESENCIA #8 PERLE COTTON

GO TO THREAD IS AURIFIL 50wt COTTON

 WOULD DIE FOR HOMEMADE POUND CAKE!

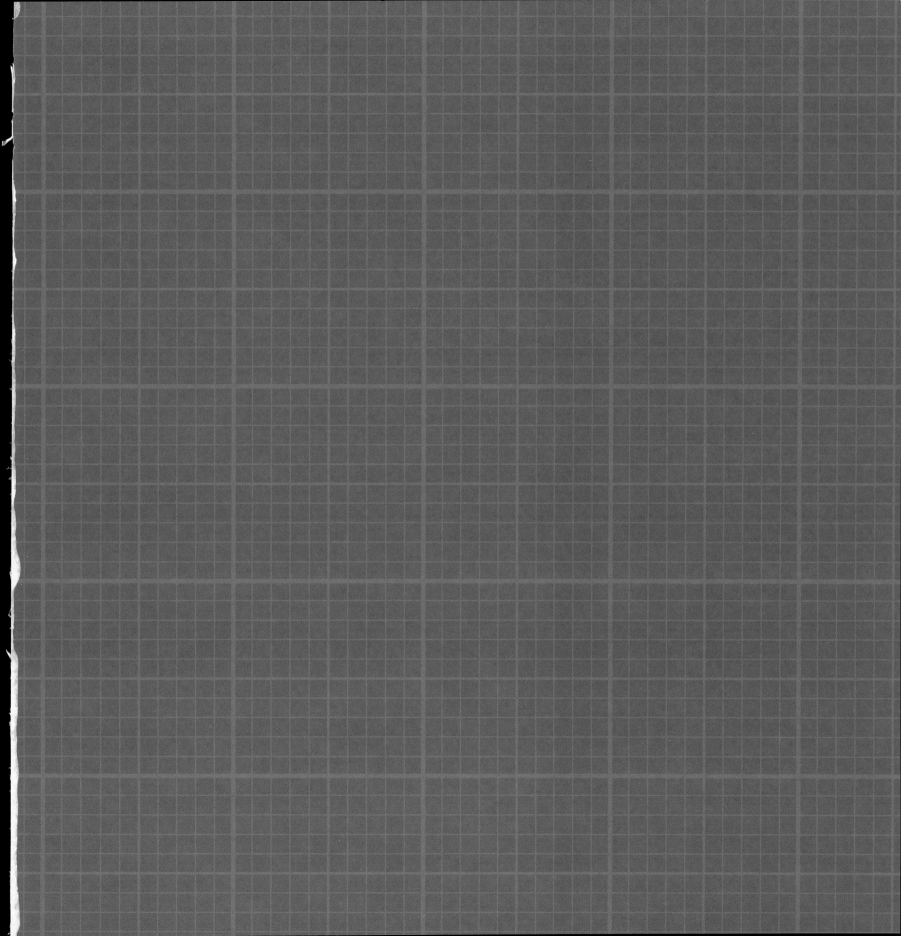

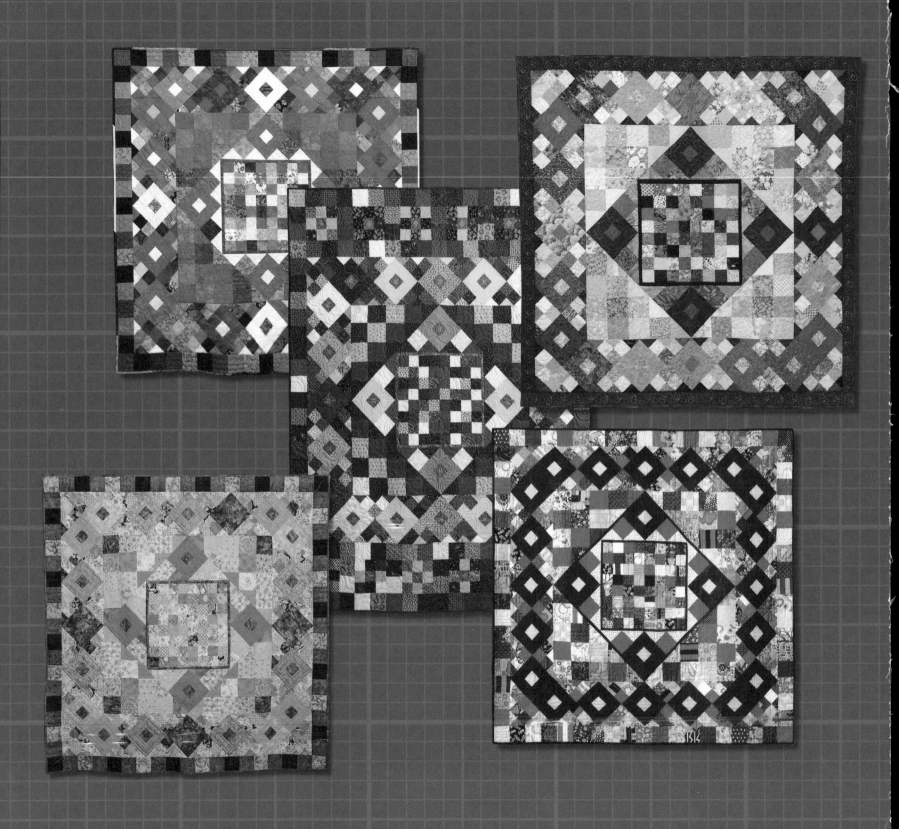